Dance
Little Ladies

Dance Little Ladies

The Days of the Debutante

Margaret Pringle

Orbis Publishing
London

Printed in England by Gale and Polden Limited, Aldershot

Endpapers : Fashionably dressed debs and their
escort pass a gypsy on their way to Ascot in 1914.

Title page : A debutante displays her train for the
camera before being presented at Court in 1932.

PICTURE ACKNOWLEDGEMENTS
Barry Swaebe; 61, 62/63, 64, 71, 72, 81, 82/83, 90, 92, 101,
110, 114/115, 118, 119, 128 bottom right, 132, 148, 154,
159, 160/161, 164, 170, 171.
Camera Press; 30 inset.
Mary Evans Picture Library; 8, 20 bottom left, 22.
Fox Photos; 30/31, 40, 44, 45 bottom, 46, 58, 61.
Courtesy of Rosina Harrison; 50 (Cecil Beaton), 55.
Tom Hustler; 82, 94, 119, 128 left, 136 bottom.
Keystone Press Agency; 73, 86, 106, 124, 158/159.
Patrick Lichfield; 7.
Mansell Collection; 2, 12.
Monitor; 115, 136 top right.
Popperfoto; 100, 136 top left, 161.
Radio Times Hulton Picture Library; Endpapers, 10/11,
19, 20, 20/21, 26, 34, 35, 36, 45 top.
Sport and General; 90/91, 106, 137, 142.
Syndication International; 128 top right, 148/149.

Contents

FOREWORD

by The Marchioness of Tavistock
(former Deb of the Year Henrietta Tiarks)

People often say when I meet them, 'Weren't you the Deb of the Year?' There really is no answer, except to nod—for what does it mean? What did it mean? It always seems strange to me that something so nebulous should still be remembered. There was no contest; we did not parade before a panel of judges and have the result announced in reverse order— I suppose it was really a Fleet Street creation.

Another question I am frequently asked is 'Did you enjoy it?' No—if I am honest, I didn't. Yet in retrospect I am glad I did it, or rather was able to do it—perhaps even was made to do it. It made me aware of many things and gave me a level on which to gauge my life. From it I realized very quickly that I do not enjoy big parties; there were sometimes two a night, which was far too many to appreciate. I found out what sort of life I didn't want, and basically I haven't changed my way of thinking— except that now, when parties are so rare, I love to be invited and find it a great pleasure to dress up and wear beautiful clothes and jewellery.

Another question often asked is 'Would you want your daughter to be a deb today?' The answer is that it would not work anymore, it would be meaningless. You cannot go to disco parties, wear make-up, smoke and go out with boyfriends before the age of seventeen and *then* be a deb. In any case, hardly anyone can afford it now, and to me anything that can only be a poor imitation is not worth doing. If I had a seventeen-year-old daughter now I would like to send her to university in America or Paris or Madrid to finish her education, and give her money to travel instead of a party, because I feel that would give her a gauge for today's life-style.

The deb era has gone; I'm glad I did it, but I would not want to relive one solitary second of it. It is, however, a beautiful visual memory, and this book provides a fascinating record of the glitter and magic of that glamorous era.

A Young Lady's
VISION
of
"THE LONDON SEASON"

INTRODUCTION

*A*continual problem for parents has always been how to rid themselves of their daughters. At the most rigorous, in Roman times, for example, it was solved by exposure. More usually, initiation ceremonies signified the daughter's coming of age and so the time at which she would be dispatched as profitably as possible. Ideally, there was a bride price. More often, there was a dowry, a reluctant allotment of some part of the family fortune so that she could marry someone of a similar social standing, often with the hope that perhaps some double marriage treaty could involve a swop of daughters and property to the benefit of both families.

In England, bargains of this sort among the landed aristocracy had long been part of the social structure. They had taken place within a small, select and easily identifiable circle, based on the court which was at the centre of power. There were those who managed to break in but they were very few and usually very rich. There was no need for a formal system of scrutiny by which the Lord Chamberlain could supervise entry to the court because the rights of those who could come were well known. Gradually the times when the court was in London, from April to the end of July – a period depending on the weather and the requirement of the hunt – produced the London season. Travel was slow and difficult; communications were poor, so that households travelled *en masse* to London, established themselves there with their daughters, and opened up their great houses for a round of parties and marriage negotiations.

This informal and yet restrictive system continued till the nineteenth century. Gradually, however, with the industrial revolution and the emergence of industrial and commercial fortunes, the system was formalized so that a limited intake of the new rich could join in. The basic concept was still to marry off daughters suitably but there was more scope as many an aristocrat was ready to welcome an alliance with the daughter of a wealthy entrepreneur. Admission to the levees and courts which had been the preserve of the aristocracy was extended to those who could find a well-connected sponsor to present them. Presentation at court marked a recognition of some degree of suitability and so a passport to marriage within the higher echelons of society as well as being part of the ritual marking the daughter's coming of age. Having made her curtsey, in white as befitted the virginal debutante, she would go on to attend the parties and numerous social events, often linked with the sporting calendar, which came to figure large in the London season.

The Royal Academy Summer Exhibition and later Covent Garden marked the beginning of the season – but neither event loomed large with the debutante, who

was never much given to attending artistic events, though she might tolerate a
visit to Glyndebourne. For her, more likely was attendance at Eton for the Fourth
of June, the school's speech day and a useful place to meet the scions of notable
families; and similarly she would visit Lords for the Eton/Harrow Match, Henley
for the Regatta. Racing was a part of the set routine, with possibly a visit to the
Derby, but more inevitably to Royal Ascot, where admission to the Royal Enclosure
was governed by the Lord Chamberlain's rules.

Apart from presentation at court, nothing was obligatory. But if your daughter
was to be invited to the coming of age parties of her contemporaries, entertainment
in kind had to be offered. In the 1920s, the charity ball became an integral part of the
season and a twirl at Queen Charlotte's, with the ceremonial cake parade, became
de rigeur. By dint of its excellent organization and its exceedingly well-connected
patronesses, this ball, which was specifically for debutantes, managed to establish
itself as an essential element of the season. For many debutantes, it was their
first ball, coming as it did at the beginning of May. During the last war, Queen
Charlotte's Ball was the only formal part of the season to survive; to some extent it
acted as a substitute for the non-existent courts, suspended for the duration of the

war. After presentation ceased in 1958, it strove, successfully for a while, to sustain this position but in later years it conceded defeat. At the end of July, society dispersed; to Scotland and Yorkshire for the grouse, to Dublin for the Horse Show, and, as sun-tans became fashionable, increasingly to Cannes and the Riviera.

The system managed to revive after the war but somehow it had become less effective as a marriage market. The girls still danced, flirted, ate strawberries and drank champagne but few of them found husbands as a result of the season. No longer did a debutante sit through season after season until she had attained this desired end, or, having failed, retire to live with a married relative in the country. After one season, most would get jobs, usually of little merit or interest. Those who did marry were no longer assured of comfort for life as divorces mounted. Times were altering; daughters were becoming less bidable; it was all too easy for the parvenu to get in, simple for a parent to find (for a fee) a sponsor for presentation at court. Dances became absurdly large, so that parents could no longer be sure their daughters were meeting the right people. Costs soared, and (as the recent lists of dances in *The Times* illustrate) the numbers of parties dwindled.

But in its time, the season had been the answer for those parents who wanted their daughters to marry eligibly. It declined as it ceased to fulfil its purpose, so that the girls who were meant to benefit latterly did not. Its ending, however, did not really affect the old families, inter-related through past generations, who will continue to meet and marry within their ranks. It has been, however, a handicap for the less established. Nothing has really replaced it and in name it staggers on. While it lasted it had some virtues, some grave disadvantages. This account is not meant to judge it, but simply to allow those who participated to say what it meant for them. For a few it was tortuous, tedious and restricting. For the majority, it was pleasurable, giving an unrepeatable chance to indulge in a summer of high frivolity with the possible bonus of entry through marriage into the ranks of the establishment.

1
THE LIGHTS GO UP AGAIN

*T*he Great War may have decimated the young men of Europe, hastened revolution in Russia and lost numerous monarchs their thrones, but in England society still centred on the court and the formal launching of young ladies into this select world survived. Coming out was still this 'glorious moment of emancipation' in the words of Loelia Ponsonby, later Duchess of Westminster, writing her memoirs. Carefully nurtured young ladies, educated by governesses in the country or at small, rather indifferent private schools, suddenly, at the age of seventeen or eighteen, put up their hair and went to dances. This overnight transformation was formally recognized when, in evening dress and train, with the three Prince of Wales feathers in their hair, they were presented at court and then went on to attend the sporting events which marked the English social calendar. Between 1930 and 1958, according to the Lord Chamberlain's Office, some 53,000 were presented, not all debutantes, as some of those making their loyal curtsey were married ladies, but the numbers show the reluctance of English society to admit change and the eagerness and determination of those making their way up to secure recognition of their arrival by observance of the old rituals.

Already there were doubts as to the validity of the process. Society had become larger and never again was it restricted to that small circle of families who genuinely knew each other and were connected by marriage, when coming out meant going to parties given by real friends in their own houses. Before the war, it had been the well-born, with some claim to court connections, who had been presented. Countess Zamoyska, who comes from an old Devon landed family and later married a Polish count, made much of this change. Her mother, she pointed out, as the daughter of a younger son, and so without a London house, was presented but did not 'do' a full season; she only attended balls given by her family or their close friends. Her step-grandmother's mother had been lady-in-waiting to Queen Adelaide. She belonged by right to court society and had the appalling fate of sitting through seven seasons until she married a man who was politically ambitious and wanted to get into court circles. This grandmother was permitted to marry him because he was very rich.

Countess Zamoyska considered that even by 1930 when she made her own debut the real justification for the season had gone:

'The whole system used to have a definite point, which was what was attractive about it. It was linked with respectability in Victoria's time, and the testing ground was the presentation at court and tickets to the Royal Enclosure at Ascot. Your mother, or whoever presented you, had to be blameless morally, at least in public, and not connected with any scandal. But the system was weakening, leaving only a vulgar marriage market based on money.

The season had started with those people who were rich enough and important enough to own a London house, which they occupied at certain times of the year according to the English sporting calendar – that is, the only times when the men could be persuaded to come to London. This meant the mating season of the pheasant, the fox, the partridge and the grouse. There was no point in bringing young girls expensively to London if there were not going to be any young men there. Then the season centred on Mayfair and on the large houses round St. James's. They opened up their houses, took off the dust-sheets and entertained their friends and relations and only their friends and relations.

Then society was extremely select and difficult to enter. Until Edward VII, there were no Jews or very few. The country families who were, so to speak, the material of the season in the 1930s did not appear in London except as cousins. You could only do the season if you were one of the great families with a great London house because you only entertained in your own home. Unless you had a house large enough for a ball, you could not have a party so you could not go to parties.'

The same point was made by Max Colombi who worked at Claridge's from 1928 to 1942, having trained at the Carlton, the Savoy and the Ritz. 'Prior to the Great War,' he said from his country retirement farmhouse in Sussex, 'the people with money and titles very seldom dined out but entertained in their own homes. The Savoy was the first luxury restaurant but it was only when the Carlton opened in 1900 – where Escoffier was Chef des Cuisines – then the Ritz in 1906 that the fashion for people to dine out became popular. Most of the coming-out dances were still held in the hostess's own London home.'

The *Tatler* hinted at the infiltration of undesirables in its social diary and in 1935, when it carried a long feature, '*The Passing Pageant, 1920–35*', in George V's Jubilee Year, decided that much had altered. 'By 1920,' its anonymous author wrote, 'the social machine, clogged and almost broken down by the long years of war and chaotic post-war hysteria, had started revolving again. By 1921, it was in top gear and going, to all appearances, smoothly. Great hostesses began entertaining, and the fixtures of the London Season again filled the Social and Personal and gossip columns of the newspapers.' However, it went on to ask, 'Did Society, as represented by those terms in pre-war days, suspect the presence of rivals and interlopers in the shape of people of undoubted wealth and doubtful birth? If they did, they kept their suspicions to themselves.'

Looking back, the *Tatler* concluded that 'during the first ten years after the War came a social revolution that upset all preconceived ideas of Society. Birth became of less importance than riches.' It had been partly because of the emergence of the professional charity organizer. 'Charitable institutions wanted money; she knew who could produce it.'

Yet, superficially at least, the debut did gradually regain some of its formality. It had lost this while young ladies retained some of the freedom they had achieved in the war years, which had also seen the granting of the vote to their elder sisters. Initially, in the 1920s, it was the gay young marrieds who called the tune with any variety of wild parties. The war had wished informality on society, and the Bright Young People took advantage of this. It was the era of flappers and bottle parties, treasure hunts and cocktails, the world of *Vile Bodies* and *Decline and Fall*. 'This was to be the great party time,' Sir Cecil Beaton recalled in his diaries, 'scarcely a night without some impromptu gathering. Quite often fancy dress taxed one's resourcefulness but added to the fun. Loelia Ponsonby, Zita, Baby and others of the Guinness contingent organized "stunt" parties, paper chases, find-the-hidden-clue races, bogus Impressionist exhibitions.'

Dancing had become the craze and nightclubs like the Diplomats Club in Bond Street, Chez Victor, Ciro's, and, smartest of all, the Embassy under Luigi became fashionable. But it was not the debutantes who went to these, or certainly not in their first season, but leaders of the smart set like Lady Diana Cooper, then one of the most photographed fashionable hostesses.

Lady Diana, the youngest daughter of the Duke of Rutland, had come out in the restricting pre-war days, and to her the war had been a time of great liberation. Still astonishingly beautiful in her eighties, she lives in Holland Park, and receives visitors sensibly from her white draped bed to which she retires not because of old age but because she considers every one should be doing their utmost to save fuel during the energy crisis.

'I suppose I was keen when I was doing the season,' she recalls, 'I was anxious to please. I still am. Coming out then was the great moment when you had long hair and you put it up with pins. I was a bit late for it because I was a precocious child, with elder sisters, so that I missed some of the excitement. I didn't have a ball; I came out at the Belvoir Hunt Ball which couldn't have been drearier.

Then there were three or four balls every night, with the dreary debutante ones in Pont Street. You sat on the stairs, never on the floor, between dances. It was considered rather common to have programmes but you always knew where you were; it would be the next dance after two. But the debutante ones were terrible and you always had your mother's eye on you to see if you were dancing with someone eligible or ineligible. And most of my friends were ineligible.

The court meant absolutely nothing to me except being presented, with the train and feathers. We weren't "in" at all, although we might have been because my grandfather had been equerry to Queen Victoria. All her girlhood, my mother had had a passion for the Princess of Wales and I had been told all about the beauty of Alexandra. But all I saw was an old woman with red hair and terrible teeth, because no one bothered about teeth in those days. When my mother had been presented, she was going to have a baby so she was given the entrée, which was a

15

lifer. This meant we could go in through the side door instead of waiting for two and a half hours in the Mall which was static with poor debutantes.'

The war had given Lady Diana much greater freedom because for the first time she was able to live away from home. 'Before that I had no liberty. I was never let out of sight and I never left the house without a friend. I would know more now if the system hadn't been like that. When the war came, I went to work in a hospital, which was back-breaking work, but I was able to live away from home. Can you imagine the happiness of that?'

The year after the war, she married Duff Cooper, a young Foreign Office clerk whom her mother considered one of the ineligibles.

The debutante season proper took some time to get going and formal presentations at court, which had been cancelled during the war, were not resumed until 1922. In the meantime, the young ladies made their debut at garden parties as they would in the years immediately after the Second World War.

The great commentator on society doings was the world-weary and ultra-snobbish Eve in the *Tatler*. In May 1919, reflecting the general feeling of hostility towards the Germans, she complained: 'Latest *here* is, you know, that last week's meat shortage (in a cold wave) happened 'cos all our spring lambs and muttons were being sent to Hun land, while the mere Britisher ruined his palate and his digestion on execrable Chinese beef. . . . But as to this Peace we're all so anxiously expectin' – the Peace season's started in all right, without waitin' for any old signin'. Weddings last week simply *never* stopped, till the Wedding March fairly rang in one's ears and the dressmakin' people drank champagne *every* night. . . . Social schemes anyway takin' no notice of any alarums and excursions without. Grand opera (such a pity there's no Chaliapin but they say he cannot leave his fourteen children) . . . the Academy, Epsom, Newmarket, Russian ballet, polo (*and* flying) beginning at Ranelagh and Hurlingham. Where, by the way, the dances they've arranged, I hear, are considered by the older members simply fearf'ly *infra dig* and out of the right and proper Hurlingham picture altogether. No pleasin' *everyone* is there?'. This year, she noted, backless sleeveless dresses were the thing.

Later the same month, she reported, 'Since last I wrote you of the tale of these dancing days, the Court's come out into the open – and's washed out the good old Courts 'pon which society's whole existence once in the good old days depended. 'Stead of those *rather* stuffy and *wickedly* expensive functions: "Their Majesties will (weather permitting) give a series of afternoon parties in the gardens of Buckingham Palace during the months of May and June, invitations to which will be equivalent to and recorded as attendance or presentation at Court as the case may be." Neat, isn't it, but not gaudy? And settles a seething question with a positively masterly simplicity . . . how to dispose of 'em, all the debs and the dowagers and the matrons and what not who for four seasons have been, like *hoi polloi*, uninvested with the necessary glamour of having been presented . . . a garden party, or rather an after-noon party in the gardens of Buckingham Palace, just simply *can't* be, at worst, a function so devastatingly dull, so enervatingly *ennuyant*, so fearf'ly feminine, so tiring, so boring as a Court . . . one won't feel as at the Courts that you weren't the only party bored stiff – the Royals were simply dead with it . . . . Settles, too, and not a moment too soon, the question of who'll be there and who won't in the Royal

Enclosure at Ascot. Where I'm told the "rush" is to be ten guineas a head . . . one and *only* idea these days . . . is to *prevent* people coming, anyway to the more exclusive shows. For a new, a *very* new – *and* rich – Society has risen up since the war and loud, Best Beloved, *very* loud is the knocking at the gate.'

To Eve's displeasure, these undesirables with more money than breeding were quite obviously able to get invited to the courts. She wrote sourly of one of the afternoon parties: 'Difficult to decide who looked worst, the matrons and "young marrieds". . . or the debs, who stood in rows in muslin and things, blue and green and purple with cold. And 'part from the clothes, 'strawdin'ry people they were, some of 'em too! Stared the poor royals positively out of countenance and to see Majesty innocently sipping its tea formed into a solid phalanx of peering pushers.'

Nonetheless, she conceded it had been quite a season, 'summer nights re-echo from dinner to breakfast to the jazz band's refrain of "Wild, Wild Women" and the rest, and a hundred dances is even the quieter young debs' dancing tot-up'.

Evelyn took over the column in 1920 and though her style was a little more restrained, her instincts were similar. In April, she commented, 'Great idea to have a season practically all the year round as you have here in Biarritz. Of course this place has been simply crowded for Easter; heaps of smart English, French, Spaniards and *naturellement* Americans. Like the poor, they are always with us . . . Awfully convenient of Paris, you know, to be on the way back from everywhere so to speak.'

She predicted a quiet season but felt that the debutante market was rather over-stocked and noted, 'The lament of the *debutante* is the extraordinary dullness of the young men.' Her own complaint was about the telephone service and has lost little over the years: 'I'm feeling just a little worn out at the present, dearest, because I've spent the whole morning writing to you with my right hand and firmly grasping the telephone receiver with my left in the vain hope of getting some of the numbers I've asked for. Every time I ask for the F.O. they tell me there's no reply. As it's already twelve it's rather hard to believe even of the F.O. but then of course, the telephone service is a Government show too isn't it?'

Originally, it had been intended to restore evening courts in 1921, but industrial problems, with the railway strike, led to their cancellation. But the other events like Ascot and Goodwood took place as usual and there was a state ball in honour of the King and Queen of the Belgians. But the next year, the pre-war system was re-established, with one minor break from tradition: 'For the first time on record,' as the *Tatler* recorded in 1935, 'came a departure from unbroken custom, when the cards of invitation had the letters "R.S.V.P." to the Lord Chamberlain printed on them . . . The step was in the interests of economy.'

An additional boost to the season was given by the budget: 'Wonderful, hasn't it been,' wrote Evelyn, 'the effect of the May Day Budget, with its blessed shilling off the income tax . . . People who have hardly entertained since the war are opening up their doors again.' The debutantes were busy getting ready for the first court on 8 June. 'Feathers,' according to Evelyn, 'are rather a difficulty with short hair, so all the bobbed ones will have to wear some sort of bandeau with the feathers fixed to it to prevent the tragedy of their falling out. The short two-yard train is rather a disappointment to the *debutantes* who are nothing if not practical, for they complain there won't be enough material in them to make any thing of them afterwards.'

17

There was another court on 14 June and soon there were five or six dances a night – but Ascot that year was arctic.

At the end of the season, in late July, London emptied. Everyone went, as Evelyn recorded, 'to peaceful country houses, with unlimited tennis and golf and bridge, and a little wild dancing to the gramophone, and many opportunities for flirtations. Or up to Scotland, perhaps, where I hear more Americans than ever have taken moors or forests, or off to some continental watering place with its promise of fine weather and smart clothes and its opportunities of indulging in a little gambling.' The hostesses that year had been Lady Irene Curzon, Lady Diana Cooper and Lady Cynthia Mosley. One slightly fraught dance had been given in Downing Street. 'Mrs Lloyd George held a dance at No 10 for her daughter Megan, who does not worry her little head about awkward political situations. I expect, though, most of the people directly concerned have been feeling very uncomfortable during the long-drawn-out honours debate.'

It was the 1924 season which attracted particular attention, for by then the first Labour government was in power with Ramsay Macdonald as Prime Minister. But any worries were premature and that year there were two state balls, one for the King and Queen of Roumania, another for the King and Queen of Italy. People seemed more concerned whether Suzanne Lenglen or Helen Wills would win Wimbledon than whether socialism would produce a complete social revolution. The courts went off satisfactorily. 'The occasion demonstrated to the full,' reported Evelyn, 'that even those who think in terms of a Communistic regime have an appreciation of the value of pomp and circumstance and the advantage of Sovereignty. At the first Court, on May 20, there were a thousand guests, mainly drawn as is usual from the diplomatic and official bodies. At the second court, guests numbered about the same, but the official section of society was in the minority.' The Eton Fourth of June celebrations clashed with the Derby. 'Odd that with a Labour Government in power we are being so very specially imperial and very specially royal this summer of 1924,' Evelyn concluded.

Even the General Strike two years later did no more than delay the dates of the courts. An emergency edition of the *Tatler* had had to be printed in Paris, and while Evelyn argued that it was the London season which helped to employ thousands of workers, she also felt a little work would not have done the debutantes any harm. 'The new dates for the Courts were promptly announced and the unusually high numbers of *debutantes*, who had begun to feel rather anxious about their high Season, will be none the worse for the job of work they put in during the Strike.'

*Below: Debs-to-be are given instruction in the correct
and incorrect ways of picking up a handkerchief at a
Kensington school of deportment in 1925. Right: Miss
V. Seymour and Mrs Stephen Ralli, suitably dressed
for Ascot in 1926. Bottom: A view of night-club life in
the 'Roaring Twenties' as seen in a social chit-chat
column in the same year.*

Left: A crowded scene on the river at the opening day of Henley Regatta in 1929. For most visitors to Henley, then as now, a day under the hot sun did not call for informality of dress.

The season had by the end of the 1920s regained much of its pre-war style and formality. Most daughters were ready to obey their parents with alacrity, and though in 1928 the voting age for women was reduced to 21, girls were being more closely chaperoned than in the immediate post-war period. 'Chaperonage had come back with a rush,' Loelia Ponsonby remembers, 'girls whose elder sisters had been hospital nurses and lorry drivers were forbidden to go to parties unless their mothers were also invited.'

Joyce Phipps, a niece of Lady Astor, made her debut in 1928 and seems to have been almost as closely chaperoned as Lady Diana Cooper was in 1911. Better known as Joyce Grenfell, she met her husband during her debutante year, as fellow guests at a houseparty. For a girl from her background at that time, the season was the only way to meet a possible husband. Joyce Grenfell has now retired from giving live performances, though she still does occasional broadcasts and has published her auto-biography. She lives in a block of mansion flats in Chelsea and recalled her debut over a cup of coffee.

'Growing up in the twenties was a matter of one night being a child and the next day you were grown up. It was as sudden as that. There was so little between the hair down (pigtails in my case) and long brown stockings and then hair up and pale beige stockings and champagne-coloured shoes, which were all the rage at that time. I came out when I was eighteen. I did the season because it was the only way to meet people. I didn't really want to do it, but once it happened I got a lot of excitement out of it because I love looking forward to things.

All the parties were in private houses, which was lovely. The big set balls in Bridgewater House and Crewe House were thrilling. The year after I came out there was a final dance at Dorchester House before it was pulled down and the hotel built in its place. This was always referred to as Resurrection Morning because people came to that party who had not been seen in London for years. All the pictures had been sold, and the carpets and most of the furniture had gone. Great swags of green leaves were hung everywhere to hide the patches where the pictures had been. That was my favourite kind of party—an all-generation party.

Debutante parties in the larger houses always included the older generation with all the ladies sitting on the chaperons' bench. The fathers never seemed to be there. They came on later from playing bridge in their clubs. The mothers sat and assessed one. One contemporary of mine was told she must never dance more than once with Mr A with whom she was in love and never less than three times with Mr B whom her mother thought was a good thing.

I was never allowed out alone. If my parents were not going to the dance, I was escorted by the family maid, who was Swiss, not much older than me, who made a lot of my dresses. She would take me in a taxi to the dinner party and then the hostess would have to see me home unless my mother or father collected me.

We did what we were told in those days. There were the nonconformists who went on to nightclubs, but I was never a breaker-outer. I was happy with things the way they were. It was the only way of meeting Reggie, who turned into my husband and is still my husband. I met him when I was seventeen and I had a very happy debutante year because he was at most of the parties I went to. I think I did most of the chasing because he was a very shy man. I always made sure there would be another occasion by asking, "Are you going to so-and-so's dance?". But I never went out alone with Reggie in the evening until we were engaged, which was the next year. I was allowed to go out with him in the day and he used to take me to Richmond Park and teach me to drive a car, his family's open high stilted Austin.

In the daytime, there were girls' luncheon parties and I went to the theatre and cinema a great deal. I could have taken A-levels in the movies when I was seventeen and eighteen. We did nothing. We were real wastrels, though I think we did a little 'good works', which was not at all a bad thing. There was a girls' club in the East End and we used to sew the most peculiar bed jackets for a hospital.

The year I came out, my grandmother gave me an allowance of £3 a month for taxis and hairdressers and it covered it. I used to get my hair done, quite well, for 4s 11d so that with a sixpence tip a pound paid for about four hairdoes. You could buy a pair of satin dance slippers at Jacques Jacobus in Shaftesbury Avenue for a guinea, have them dyed whatever colour you wanted and pick them up the same afternoon.

All my dresses were made at home except my coming out dress, which my aunt gave me, and my presentation dress. I had dresses made in cotton organdie in pale colours, very pretty, which could be laundered and pressed. Between May the 3rd and the 23rd of July, I went to a dance every weekday night except Friday and Saturday. I didn't actually have a dance myself although I shared my cousin's dance. I did not really contribute anything but I stood in line with her to receive people. My dress came, I think, from Vionnet and was pale pink net, with pale blue picquot-edged taffeta ribbon in loops with roses.

When I was presented, I had a dress from Norman Hartnell given to me by my grandmother. It was white chiffon, princess line, with a border round the hem of picquot-edged ribbon so it stood out, and of course feathers and white gloves. I sat in my grandmother's car in the Mall with all those people watching. The insensitivity of it strikes me today but I don't think there was a sense of envy. I think people enjoyed others' good fortune. I don't remember King George or Queen Mary. What I remember is Reggie rather casually happening to walk down the Mall and passing me in the car. It was very romantic. He was courting me in silence because people didn't declare themselves much in those days unless you could actually hope to get married, and Reggie didn't have any money and he didn't have a job.

The season was probably tough on people who didn't know many people.

Hostesses did take trouble to see that you met people and if you were standing by the door and not dancing, they would introduce you to a young man who was also not dancing. But still, a great many people spent a great deal of time in the ladies' room, powdering their noses when they weren't actually invited to dance. We only occasionally had programmes, which was rather amusing but also rather frightening in case you did not get asked. But I was so passionately interested in watching people that I didn't mind not being asked to dance because I liked to sit at the side and watch. I didn't have a stream of young men behind me like some of the girls, but I did have plenty of friends.

We were pretty snobbish, I suppose, and if there were two dances one evening and one was in a grand place and the other somewhere like Upper Phillimore Gardens, one was rather inclined to go from duty to Upper Phillimore Gardens and then go on to the next one.

There was a certain amount of gatecrashing. There was a very famous case at Bridgewater House when Cecil Beaton and one of his sisters were asked to leave. It wasn't entirely their fault because they had been asked to a dinner party and then taken on to the dance. But properly, if you were asked to a dinner party and were not invited to the dance you should refuse the dinner party.

But the season had changed since the First World War and was not so exclusive. Society had opened up and really meant anybody. Before the War, it was tiny and everyone did know everybody. My grandmother was a very old-fashioned type and she thought it was a disgrace to be in the press. Once my photograph was in the *Tatler* when I designed some dresses for a friend who was a dancer and my grandmother did not like that at all. Later, there was an exhibition of painting at the Academy and a portrait Sargent had done of my grandmother was used to publicize the exhibition. The poster was on railings and on the underground. I could just imagine my grandmother spinning. I can remember it being thought quite shocking when people started to advertise Pond's Cold Cream. That was frowned on.

The season was really quite fun. I enjoyed everything except Ascot – my idea of total boredom is a race meeting, and I never went there again. I did not enjoy the weekends very much because they were inclined to be a bit formal and nearly always in big houses, and my close friends did not have big country houses. It was the luck of the draw whom you met at weekends. Of course if Reggie was going to be there it did not matter where we were going. Then on July 23rd my parents sent me to America for three months because although they were very fond of Reggie they felt I must have a chance to meet other people. They sent me to stay with an aunt but I couldn't stick it and came back after two months. Next year we got married.'

2

DEPRESSION? WHAT DEPRESSION?

*I*t is surprising, looking back, that the political and economic events so little affected the outward observance of the season. Throughout, however, there was a feeling that the season was different from pre-war days. Eve, taking up her column again, reflected, in May 1929, 'It really ought to be given some kind of new name now that it is a very different thing from the formal and rather grim affair of the past, so very much monopolised by match-making mothers with marriageable daughters.' But whatever changes there had been, it flourished despite the growing financial crisis.

Der Rosenkavalier with Bruno Walter and Lotte Lehmann opened the opera season and, despite the pending election, Easter saw the usual English visitors heading for Le Touquet, 'to fortify themselves for the coming struggle.' The 1929 election did put a temporary stop to debutante dances. 'The election of course,' wrote Eve, 'meant a complete cessation of social activities for the whole of last week. It was the poor debutantes who suffered most, for their dances were definitely off, while those of the slightly older generation found compensation in a few on-the-spur-of-the-moment parties, in the interval of strenuous electioneering. On second thoughts, though, the week's rest from late nights was probably for the good of the debutantes' looks.'

Ramsay Macdonald emerged from the struggle as Prime Minister, succeeding Stanley Baldwin. On election night, 'There were dozens of familiar faces to be seen at the Savoy . . . After a time a good many went on to Mr Selfridge's party. As usual, the organisation was above criticism and Mr Selfridge, always the perfect host, greeted all his guests with a charming smile and "I'm so glad you were able to come!" . . . always on the look-out to see everybody had everything they wanted. This without exaggeration; one could send telegrams and cables without paying and even telephone New York.'

There were still great balls in the great London houses although gradually many were being pulled down. One such was given by Lady Londonderry at Londonderry House. This was one of the last great balls of the pre-war type, the all-generation ball with the debutantes very much in the background. As Eve described it: 'It was one of the real old-fashioned balls. Duchesses and dowagers, laden with tiaras and dog collars, flowed up the magnificent staircase, followed by meek debutante daughters, in tulle dresses of pastel shades. Cabinet ministers, defeated and otherwise, leant against marble pillars and discussed the political situation with ex-members of Parliament and countless couples waltzed to the strains of Ambrose's Blue Danube. Lady Londonderry, at the top of the stairs, looked very regal in a white taffeta dress and a magnificent tiara of diamonds . . . It was a wonderful sight and one couldn't help feeling proud to think that this is practically the only country where such balls can still be given.'

The Depression may have been getting worse but in the high season there were still several balls a night. Costs were astonishingly low. A dance for 400 guests might set the host back £200 or £300. In 1933, for example, Searcy's, then as now one of the top catering firms, could provide supper at a ball for 9s a head, with breakfast at 9d, and this would be bacon and eggs, kedgeree and perhaps filletted kippers. Until the 1960s, supper as well as breakfast was always provided at a dance. In 1933, non-vintage champagne was 10s a bottle, cigarettes 4s a hundred. Wages were low. When Margaret Whigham married Charles Sweeny, the two detectives hired for the whole day to watch the wedding presents earned £2 10s each. For a ball, the link man for the door could be hired for 10s 6d; the cloakroom maid earned the same. The special announcer and the cocktail mixer were the most expensive human items at £1 1s a head; the managing waiter received 15s 6d. These sums were reflected in other costs. At the Whigham/Sweeny reception, the tent, with a carpet and lined with pleated art muslin in yellow and cream, cost £20. Searcy's could send tea for thirty guests and the two waiters to serve it down to Ascot for five guineas.

With the support of the enthusiastic Lady Cunard, the opera season at Covent Garden continued. In 1930, there was Strauss, Wagner, Flotow, Montemezzi, Debussy, and 'of course,' as the *Sketch* put it, Puccini and Verdi. At the Royal Academy, there were pictures by Augustus John, including his portrait of Tallulah Bankhead, and both Laura Knight and Sir John Lavery exhibited works. But these were not really debutante events. They left the opera to the hostesses, preferring to go to the movies and, later in the year, Noel Coward's new comedy, *Private Lives*, in which he starred with Gertrude Lawrence.

Queen Charlotte's Ball was one of the charity dances which was becoming accepted as a regular seasonal event the debutante would attend, though it did not have the importance its survival during the next war was to attach to it. But that May, the *Tatler* reported, 'All the prettiest "buds" seemed to have been assembled at the May Fair Hotel last week when Queen Charlotte's Birthday Ball raised a substantial sum of money for Queen Charlotte's Hospital at Hammersmith. The great moment of the evening was when thirty-one charming Maids of Honour all dressed in white, and heralded by trumpeters of the Royal Horse Guards, drew into the ballroom a birthday cake big enough for a regiment of Carneras. Lady Diana Cooper . . . was the Dame d'Honneur in this decorative procession . . . on the cake of which

28

HRH Princess Beatrice cut the first slice were 186 electric candles representing the number of years since the birth of Queen Charlotte, the first royal patron of the hospital which bears her name.'

This was the year Margaret Whigham came out. Later Mrs Charles Sweeny and then Duchess of Argyll, she, like Henrietta Tiarks in 1957, achieved public notice simply because she was a deb, admittedly one who was richer and more beautiful than most of the others. She became a national figure whose doings were reported in the daily press as well as in society journals. There were even rumours, which she has always vehemently denied, that she had a publicity agent, and it was said that her father, a Scots/American who had made a great deal of money, put down £1000 to see that her launching was properly noticed. She thinks that she and a few of her contemporaries achieved this attention simply because they were more sophisticated than the previous deb generation. But certainly, when she married her first husband, Charles Sweeny, an American golfer, in 1933, crowds gathered outside the Brompton Oratory as if it had been a royal wedding.

That year, Atalanta, the columnist of *Harpers' Bazaar*, which had started the previous October, commented, 'Most of the debutantes to be presented at Court have already enjoyed the dances and balls so that their curtsey to Royalty is a formality which marks their entry into a society they have already entered.' In its 1935 article, the *Tatler* was to comment, 'The years 1928-31 provided some lovely new-comers into society. There were the Beaton sisters, . . . Lady Bridgett Poulett. There was Margaret Whigham, so sweet by nature that publicity failed to spoil her.' And in 1930 they had already picked her out: 'Margaret Whigham must I think be awarded the prize of this year's dazzle of debutantes. Her black and yellow dress [at Ascot] only helped to confirm a pretty general opinion.'

Even today, the Duchess of Argyll is still considered a figure worthy of mention in most gossip columns, whether it is her attendance at the Red Cross Ball being photographed in the *Tatler* or newspaper reports about whether the owners of her Grosvenor Street house would be entitled to take away her lease because she personally, for a large fee, conducts visitors round the house. It is one of the very few private houses left in Mayfair, with a large ornately furnished drawing room, scattered with rich trinkets. The Duchess, despite the trials and tribulations of her divorce from the Duke of Argyll when she was accused of being an immoral woman by the judge in his summing up, is a remarkably ageless beauty. She remembers her own debut with unqualified enthusiasm:

'I of course looked forward to the season', says the Duchess, 'and it was even better than I had expected it to be. It was gay and exciting and I enjoyed meeting new people. The intention was to enable the mothers to introduce their daughters to other sons and daughters of the same age. But if the first season was good, the second and third were even better because by then you had established your own friends and you were allowed to dine out.

The debutantes of my year were an innovation. We were much more sophisti-cated, we were attractive and good talkers. We could get on with people, whereas before the debutantes had often been not very interesting people. Before my day, it had been the young married women who made the fashion and the debutantes who had upset it with their blue tulle and pink bows. But then we, Rose Bingham,

Below: The queue in the Mall for presentations at court in 1933. Inset: Miss Margaret Whigham, later to become the Duchess of Argyll, waits her turn to enter Buckingham Palace in 1930. She was one of the most famous debs of her time.

Lady Bridget Poulett and myself, arrived on the scene, very sophisticated and looking much older than we were. At 17, I looked far older than my age and did my darndest to do so. I had had an international upbringing and had been with older people a great deal. I had been practically "out" for a long time. For the first time, debutantes started to get a lot of publicity. But I never had a press agent, although there were rumours that I did. Why should I want one? My father would rather have jumped over the moon. I think it was simply that we happened to come between the pin-up girls and the marvellous models like Fiona Campbell-Walter. But now glamour is out of fashion.

The actual presentation was very awe-inspiring, very very memorable. But you cannot look back and I think it would be out of date today. And of course, people haven't the money. When I was presented, crowds used to watch because they enjoyed looking at pretty people and pretty clothes. There was no antipathy at all, everyone was very kind and there was no single ugly note, no anger at all despite the Depression. They gawped, but in a nice way, and we were pretty butterflies.

Of course, sometimes the papers poked fun. I remember when Britain went off the gold standard the next year, the *Daily Express* wrote: "As an example to the girlhood of Britain, the lovely Margaret Whigham has decided, in the interests of economy, to have her hair re-set only once a fortnight in future, and to stop wearing stockings in the evening. On the other hand, to stimulate trade, she has bought four new evening dresses."

I had been to finishing school in Paris so I did know a lot of girls who came out with me, even though we had been abroad so much. But of course it was much easier for me when young Frances [her daughter, now Duchess of Rutland] came out because she had been at boarding school in England and I had been living here.

You needed at least six ball dresses and day dresses, half a dozen cocktail dresses and of course four outfits for Ascot. And you did wear everything out because there was the "little season" in the autumn. But it really was not so expensive. You could get a really beautiful dress, all hand-embroidered, for £18. I can remember being really shocked when my wedding dress cost £52.

I took a risk by having my own coming-out dance very early on, on May 1st. It was at 6 Audley Square where my parents lived. But I never really went into the "game" business – if you ask me, I'll ask you – over parties. I just invited pretty attractive girls. Then the second year, I had a dance at my parents' house near Ascot which was really more fun.

There would be six or eight parties a night and you would weed them out and not go to the ones where you did not know the hosts. There were lists to help mothers who lived in the country and were out of touch. People were paid – so-called "ladies" – to get these girls invited to as many parties as possible. But if the mothers did live in the country, you didn't think any the worse of them for it, and it was useful for the American debutantes also. But once the girl was taken in and accepted, she became part of the scene, and she *would* be if she were gay and pretty. But there were the girls who came out who promptly "went in" again. If you were plain and dreary, there was nothing which could be done.

The trouble with the big dances was the programmes, though I evolved my own technique for dealing with them. Early on, I would agree to dance with anyone who asked me so that there would be no blanks. When my favourite beau appeared, I would ruthlessly fill in my programme again and pretend to the first boy that I had made a mistake over where I thought we had arranged to meet. Sometimes the music was bad but I was never bored, because I never am bored, period. If the parties were boring, you wouldn't stay. It wasn't really the dances I enjoyed but the restaurant life. I much preferred to scuttle off to a nightclub, although I would have been furious if I had not been invited to the dances. What I really enjoyed was going to the Embassy Club, which until then had been for the smart young marrieds. I was the first debutante to be made a member there and I practically lived there. I used to lunch and dine there the whole time. You always had to go off to a nightclub in fours, but often my parents would take us on because they would get bored with the dances.

Mothers, of course, were meant to go everywhere with their daughters and I think some of them found it quite fun because they hadn't been anywhere for a long time and they had a good time just talking. But my mother wouldn't do that and if she did not want to go somewhere she would just make me promise to go home in our car. You never went anywhere if you were not invited. Viscount Selby had asked me to go with him to a ball that Viscountess Cowdray was giving in Mount Street, saying he had been asked to bring a partner. But when we got there, Lady Cowdray asked me if I had been invited and asked me to leave. My parents were furious and made her apologize. After all, I was not a tramp coming in from the street.

I didn't do a lot of weekending. I preferred to go to my parents' house at Ascot. Anyhow, one was pretty tired by the end of the week. I was expected to be up and dressed every morning by nine, although of course you could have a nap after lunch. I only went to the sporting events if they were social. I went to the Derby and Ascot because they were glamorous and you could go there without looking at a horse. I went to Lords, to the Eton and Harrow match, but you certainly did not need to see any cricket.

It was the large private houses, like Brook House and Warwick House, which were the most beautiful. And of course, when I came out, there was always a member of the royal family there. The Prince of Wales and the Duke of Kent were both bachelors and they were so charming they lit up the room when they came in. But Prince Charles is away so much, he prefers nightclubs anyway, and Princess Anne only likes horses. Princess Margaret is really the only one who gets about.

When young Frances came out, the season was on the road to change. I think the girls took life much more seriously than we did. By then, there were no evening courts, so she was presented in a short dress. We had her coming-out dance at Claridge's, for 800 people, with dinner for 100 before hand. In those days, people loved a pipe band so we had one of those and then Tim Clayton's band which was marvellous. And a cabaret. When I came out, I had been dressed by Norman Hartnell and Victor Stiebel, but she was dressed entirely in Paris.

By then chaperoning was really over. What worried the mothers was that the girls might go home with someone who was a bit tight, it was not about morals. But I think the girls were awfully sensible. One mother would take about 20 girls

Left: Lady Bridget Poulett and Mr Michael Menzies arrive at the Dorchester for the 1931 Queen Charlotte's Ball. Below: The Maids of Honour bring in the giant cake at the same ball.

to the dance and if it were me, I would not necessarily stay to the bitter end. But it was nice for the girls to have someone older to talk to and perhaps to ask where the cloakroom was. But they always seemed to have a nice time because I always asked the pretty girls and I put Frances onto it to see that everyone was all right.

These days everything has changed so much. We used to go to so many dances and film first nights when people would wear white fox fur and what-have-you. Now no one dresses up. No one wears ball dresses, just those long dresses which are not really dressy. I miss the glamour. I think people look so drab these days and it isn't a question of money; they don't care, they want to be sloppy. The season is more for foreigners and a useful way to repay hospitality. Foreigners come over for the Derby, Ascot and Cowes, and God bless them for that. Now the season is over. If I had a daughter of 17, I would take her travelling. She would meet young people anyway. They go to colleges and universities, my God. I never wanted a job. I didn't want a career. I was just grateful I didn't have to have one.' Some, of course, were more critical, like Countess Zamoyska, who was Margaret Whigham's contemporary:

'The season was already in its decadence. Only a few of the great London houses remained and it was already vulgarized and run by ambitious mothers and worse daughters in a sort of female network. My mother did not "do" the season because she was only the daughter of a younger son, but what small contact she had had with the great London world put her off it to such a degree – she was shy and unsociable – that when it was thought necessary for me to do the season, she went to Assisi to contemplate. I was left in charge of a poor female relation (I wonder what has happened to poor female relations. They used to be everywhere but I expect now they have splendid careers) who lived in the house with me to make it respectable.

The season centred round the dreadful lunch parties where, before the last course was even finished, girls would be whipping out engagement books and on that you could go to three or four balls a night. But no one introduced you. It was so typically English; even though it was no longer a small select society where everyone did know everyone, it was assumed to be the case. So if you did not know anybody, you met nobody.

The only proper way to go was in dinner parties. Women who were giving the dances would ask other women who were giving dances to have dinner parties on a "cutlet for cutlet" basis. They would list the girls to be invited but often it was up to the mothers to invite the young men. The female side was very organized and competent. Most of the girls had been to finishing schools in France and they knew each other from school. They did not go to schools like Wycombe Abbey, nor Roedean, nor Cheltenham, which were for education, but the fashionable private schools which have mostly disappeared.

At some of the parties there would be the girls from the great families still lingering on, and a very few did still have London houses. Then there were the enormously rich Jews like the Sassoons, Rothschilds and Raphaels, all entertaining on a very lavish scale and on the whole being more interesting because they would go to Paris and do the season there so at least they had moved about a bit. And the Americans were starting to arrive in shoals.

But there were very few foreigners. I made the mistake of trying to launch an Italian beauty I had met at finishing school. But no Englishman would look at her because he didn't know her name and she didn't have a grouse moor. So this beautiful girl – she was the daughter of a banker and had people queuing to dance with her in Italy – was wallflowering in London. In the end she had to be sent home.

I had really wanted to go to Oxford but my family thought it would put a disastrous blight on my possibility of marrying so I spent three summers sitting in rented houses in London in the best months of the year. I did make some good female friends and it does mean that the rest of your life you know people where-ever you go. The men on the whole were young officers in the Brigade of Guards or the bank clerks, as we called them, who were not so smart – which is something that has changed. The bank clerks were very young and learning a profession so they were delighted to have an excellent dinner laid on for them.

We still had chaperons, but often they did duty for several girls. It was awfully dull for them because there were no men. In the old days when there were proper parties the fathers had come, but in my day it was entirely for the girls, and the mothers talked to each other. Usually it was token chaperonage but some mothers were very strict. My eldest brother's future mother-in-law hadn't been in London since she was a girl and she still applied the same rules. She took him aside and said to him: "You have danced twice with my daughter and I think that is enough." He was so impressed he proposed immediately.

I do remember Margaret Whigham saying at a girls' luncheon party that she was not allowed to go shopping on her own, but that was rather putting the clock back. The inference anyway was that she was so beautiful that she might have come to harm if she had gone out alone.

We used to go around a lot in gangs. We didn't get up till midday and then we met for girls' luncheon parties and then went round and left our bread-and-butter letter for the night before. Then the entertaining started at about six o'clock with cocktail parties. The rest of the day was spent with fittings and having one's hair washed. One friend of mine had very beautiful hair and she had it washed and set every day, which is like a film star today.'

It was not quite like the old days when it was simply not done to be seen in London in August – Christopher Petherick, joint managing director of Searcy's, remembers his father describing how people would get in a month's supply of food, close their windows and put up their shutters to bolster the pretence they had gone away. But the majority of London society still did go, perhaps to Scotland or Le Touquet, though the South of France was becoming increasingly popular for the dashing. Mariegold, reporting from Le Touquet for the *Sketch*, noted it was a bit behind the South of France on the fashion front: pyjamas for the beach were not yet *de rigueur*, although several ladies were looking extremely smart in the cricket cap which was very much in for *le sport*.

Eve took an optimistic view of things in May 1931: 'Here in London we are a little brighter. One reason is the return of the Princes . . . the Budget is no longer the unknown horror . . . the opening of Covent Garden Opera was almost impudently glorious. Everyone with a jewel wore it, gloves were on every hand and furs abounded also . . . there is no doubt that tiaras are very becoming, and have an enormous effect on deportment. You cannot loll and wilt while supporting the family jewels.' She noted that debutantes preferred the smaller dances as 'the large and more alarming affairs . . . rather swamp the shy and diffident.'

In September that year, Lady Sibell Lygon, one of several sisters who were friends of Evelyn Waugh, started to edit a monthly column in *Harpers' Bazaar*, to which Evelyn Waugh and Nancy Mitford were now regularly contributing short stories and articles. Lady Sibell edited this 'Vanity Fair' column till the end of the 1930s, commenting on society trends – 'No one could call the Ritz dull,' she would write. In June 1932, she described an unlikely figure on the social scene, the young Nye Bevan. 'Another interesting member of this group,' she reported, 'is Mr Bevan, a Socialist from Wales. He firmly believes in and lives up to his convictions, even if at times he slightly over-reacts. I once saw him at a London ball and there, among all London society dressed up to the nines, was Mr Bevan in a lounge suit and carrying it off with the greatest success. I have seen him on one occasion brush back his unruly mob of black hair – with one eye on the mirror over the fireplace. Apart from that one small conceit he does not think of himself and is completely natural. Sometimes he is rather apt to boast of his humble origins and to make a virtue of the lowly estate of his relations. I told him a Duke's son could not boast more proudly of his origins. He assured me that Duke's sons don't have the same distinction.'

The Embassy Club remained *the* place to go, as Lady Diana Cooper remembers: 'It was very smart, in Bond Street, and there was dancing. It was like a party in a private house. It was "all right". The Prince of Wales was there nearly every night. He was very glamorous, with shining gold hair. I only got to know him when he was courting Mrs Simpson. The Duke of Kent was not so "in".'

By 1932 the Depression had become very serious, but *Harpers' Bazaar* encouraged its readers in January 1933 with a page of New Year's Resolutions. Number Three read: 'To drop from your conversation for ever the words "crisis" and "depression". In fact to be sufficiently *grande dame* to stop talking about money altogether.' And on the whole, society seems to have followed that advice. In its 1935 article, the *Tatler* listed some of the outstanding hostesses and parties of the time. There were the dinners given by American Mrs James Corrigan, and Mrs Ronald Greville continued her habit of entertaining celebrities, both British and foreign, at her house in Charles Street and her country home, Polesden Lacey. 'Lady Londonderry keeps her place as the premier political hostess and appreciates the value of pageantry better than any other woman in London. Kings and Queens come to Londonderry House, so do poets, artists, actors, actresses, authors and many other people.'

But the *Tatler* concluded that in the fifteen years since 1920 the character of the season had altered:

'With the exception of Courts, State Balls, and Royal dinner parties, entertaining has . . . undergone a complete change. No one wants to go to big gatherings. The most popular form of party giving is a snack meal with a cinema to follow . . . the Charity Ball too is a post-war innovation. It was also responsible for the spate of "pageants" . . . the Charity Ball has largely replaced the dignified private dances which great hostesses in London gave during pre-war seasons, when debutantes were launched into society at dances where the guests included distinguished people of all ages, and the uninvited guest problem . . . had not arisen. Today, debutante dances are gatherings of very young people, the girls hardly out of the schoolroom, the men scarcely older. Hostesses keep a careful check on the names of those likely to be entertaining. Invitations are issued only to those from whom invitations are likely to be received in return. Chaperons willing to provide dinners for a certain number of guests are handed lists of names of those whom the hostess would like included in her party . . . the cutlet for cutlet principle is firmly established . . . as a means of introducing eligible young men to attractive girls, these dances are useless. Eligible young men shun them, and what after all is a *debutante's* dance for but to bring young people together with a view to matrimony later on? The fashion for chaperons, who were more or less out of date after the war, has been revived. Hence the numerous tired mothers who line the walls of the ballroom nightly when the season is in full blast.'

3

THE LATER THIRTIES

The year 1935 was George V's Silver Jubilee, celebrated by a state drive, a service of thanksgiving in St Paul's, and junketings throughout the country. The English season flourished along its traditional lines. In February, according to Lady Sibell Lygon in *Harpers' Bazaar*, the English were skiing in Kitzbühel and St Anton 'with dashes to St Moritz to acquire ultra-cosmopolitan atmosphere or to Klosters to join up with the large party of English there. London was brightened by jolly boy-and-girl dances held during the holidays, which started the Jubilee year off in fine style; by the visit of Eddie Cantor, who wisecracked at the opening night of the new cabaret show at the Dorchester, to the delight of a huge roomful of stage celebrities; by the opening of Pruniers in St James's Street. Country house parties were on pre-war scale and enjoyed numbers of hunt balls, lots of good hunting and an immense ball at Belvoir Castle. So many people were invited and came that, huge as Belvoir is, the Duchess of Rutland had to take an hotel at Grantham to use as an overflow! All the Rutland clan were present; the Tennants and Asquiths are related and all the Pagets too, as well as the Charteris family, so they made a big party to start with. Belvoir, floodlit, looked like a fairy castle perched up in the clouds.'

It was becoming more difficult to ignore events on the continent and the growth of fascism, but the main events of the 1935 season continued as normal. Miss Betty Vacani, who in subsequent years was to teach generations of *gauche* debutantes to curtsey with at least a degree of grace, was herself presented that year:

'I was at the last court George V gave, with, of course, the feathers and the train. You had to curtsey, making sure you got up on the correct foot to avoid your train, take three steps sideways and curtsey again and then as you walked out, you put out your left arm and the usher put your train over it. I was presented by my aunt, Marguerite Vacani. They called out her name, Mrs Lesley Rankin, and then "and to be presented," and you followed in the lady who was presenting you. With the train, you often carried a fan or flowers as well so it was difficult. You had to warn the girls not to wear diamante buckles, and to wear comfortable shoes because there was a lot of standing around. I always remember George V's piercing blue eyes. After the presentations, the King and Queen walked down the line of debutantes and dowagers and as they passed every one curtsied. It looked like the wind blowing through the flowers.'

It was Marguerite Vacani who had started to teach dancing, and her first royal patron had been Princess Alice of Athlone. Miss Vacani still continues the classes and her pupils have included the Queen and Princess Margaret and George and Gerald

Lascelles. In the pre-war days, she says, 'We always used to have a matinee in one of the London theatres and one of the acts was always the debutantes in their long dresses. They would do something very simple, just with a little fan or a flower because often they were not very adept. But of course now there are no more presentations and there is hardly any formal dancing. Even at Princess Anne's wedding dance there were very few formal dances.'

The occasional political note did creep in. Lady Sibell Lygon lamented in October 1935, 'The Little Season's plans have been very much interfered with by the Abyssinian crisis and the prospect of a General Election. One young man who has been working extremely hard is Mr Ronald Cartland who is standing somewhere in Birmingham.' But in general the disruption was not very serious. The Duke of Gloucester's wedding to the daughter of the Duke of Buccleuch, 'a fine horsewoman' according to the *Queen*, went off in fine style on 6 November. Her trousseau, like that of Margaret Whigham two years before, came from Norman Hartnell. In the same issue, the *Queen* gave advice on how to dress a debutante for £56 10s 6d. Although this did not include the court dress, it did provide a fairly comprehensive wardrobe which included a woollen dress for $4\frac{1}{2}$ guineas, an overcoat for $8\frac{1}{2}$ guineas, an evening dress in shaded chiffon and a waist length sable-dyed squirrel fur for $8\frac{1}{2}$ guineas—all in all, a wardrobe 'that would meet a variety of occasions with distinction and chic.'

Election night, Lady Sibell reported in the December issue of *Harpers' Bazaar*, 'was celebrated with the usual monster party at Mr Selfridge's store. The Manners and the Pagets came early and went on to Lady Diana Duff Cooper's own party'. The Conservatives were returned with a strong majority, so that Baldwin, who had taken over from Ramsay MacDonald earlier in the year, remained Prime Minister.

Early the next year, on 20 January 1936, George V died, and the popular Prince of Wales acceded as Edward VIII. Throughout the year the rumours of his liaison with Mrs Simpson were growing, but these were tactfully ignored by the press and the actual abdication crisis only became public knowledge on 2 December when the press broke their silence. By 11 December the Duke of York had become George VI. On 10 December the *Queen*'s cover had been a portrait of the Duchess of York. On the 17th, it had a special 'God Save the King and Queen' cover with the Duchess of York now Queen Elizabeth. Hitler had marched into the Rhineland in March and the Spanish Civil War had broken out in July, but the debutantes danced on. The most radical change was that more and more of the dances were held in hotels. This was partly because fewer people had large London houses, but even those who had, as Max Colombi points out, did not like the disruption that holding a dance in their

42

own home involved. When the Dorchester was built on the site of Dorchester House it had a large ballroom, although it was not considered a fashionable venue until after the war. Claridge's was the place, and also the Hyde Park because of its position and access to the park. But the dances were extravagant and at one dance £500 was spent on flowers alone.

Mr Colombi recalls the dances at Claridge's in the 1930s:

'The average number of guests would be between 400 and 500. First there would be the dinner parties: the hostess would probably have twenty or so to dine, either in her house or in the hotel before the dance—the dinner not too elaborate, to finish in time for the hostess to receive the dance guests at about 10.30 p.m. The new ballroom at Claridge's opened in 1932 and was the fashionable place. It did not lend itself to major alteration and the decor would inevitably be floral; Constance Spry was the outstanding florist.

There was a running buffet throughout the evening in an adjoining small ballroom and champagne and soft drinks were served the whole time. Incidentally, hard drinks were never encouraged. Supper would invariably be served in another of the adjoining small ballrooms and would consist of, say, *Consommé Madrilène*, *Filet de Sole Duglèré*, Quails in Aspic, *Suprême de Volaille Princesse*, and an elaborate sweet, with champagne or lager. Breakfast was always offered towards the end of the dance, after 2 AM, and would consist of bacon and eggs, kidneys, salmon kedgeree, and coffee. Consumption of champagne was approximately a bottle a head, the price being about 25s a bottle.'

Naturally, an hotel cost more than going to a private caterer, and at Claridge's dinner would have been about 25s a head.

When Gill Jackson came out in 1937, she was presented to the new King, George VI. Whatever fears the *Tatler* may have expressed on the continued usefulness of the season as a marriage market were not necessary in her case. Very early in her coming-out year she met her future husband, now Sir Francis Sandilands and chairman of the Commercial Union. They have a comfortable penthouse flat in Chelsea and an excellent cook. Although Sir Francis's niece was a debutante in 1975, Lady Sandilands does not consider the system has any relevance today. Nonetheless, there was much she enjoyed about her own coming-out year:

'I find it hard to make a fair assessment of the season because I met my husband at the second dance I went to, so that I loved the dances if Francis was going to be there. But he generally only stayed till dance eight. I think he came chiefly for the food.

It had occurred to me not to do the season because I had spent a year and a half in France and I did think of writing to ask if I could stay on. But then I had a slight up-and-downer with my chums and I thought I might as well come home and do it. I was very young anyway. I don't think people realize how easily you are led when you are young. Then, we did what our parents wanted, now, in the same way, young people are often led into militance. The season was the usual thing to do and I didn't think of it as a waste of money. I never questioned any of that. My mother was a widow and very "anti" my doing anything at all. She liked to have me at home as a kind of unpaid curate, so it was a nice way for me to fill the time.

Far left: Madame Vacani instructs debs-to-be in the proper technique of the curtsey. Below left: Lady Zia Wernher, Miss Georgina Wernher, the Countess of Airlie and Lady Jean Ogilvy leave for the palace in 1937. Left: The glamorous Prince of Wales with Mrs Simpson at Ascot in June 1935, six months before his accession. Below: Ginger beer and picnic lunches for young ladies at Ascot in 1935.

I think the worst aspect of the whole carry-on was the way we spent our days. It was absolute folly. We lived in the country but my mother had taken a little house in Chester Row and we went there with my mother's lady's maid. There was acres of time during the day. Sometimes I would go and see my married sisters who lived in London and collect their children from school. Or I might lunch with friends and go to an exhibition. But by and large our time was completely wasted. There was not time to get involved in a job or in learning something, although this did not worry me. The season sapped your energy and initiative because you only met people who were doing exactly the same thing.

The other most ghastly thing about being a deb was that you only saw your own age-group, which was no standard to go by at all. There were dances every night and on Fridays in the country, though I did not usually weekend because my mother liked having me around. But we never saw anybody interesting. Oh, and those godawful tea parties. But the food was always lovely, though I didn't eat very much. But we had endless smoked salmon sandwiches and quails and delicious black cherries. We had those dance programmes with their silly little pink or blue pencils which were hopeless for anything else. It was terribly embarassing if you had to show your card and it was blank. It was fraught with difficulty, but if you were really hating it you could always go to your mother. But people were less outspoken than they are now, and you tended not to say that you weren't enjoying something.

We were always chaperoned. My mama would go to the dinner party and on to the ball. The mothers would sit along the wall and chat, although there were the dashing mothers who would come on from Covent Garden. I think there was much more competition between the mothers than between the girls. I am sure my mother got more out of it than I did because she led a very sheltered life as a widow.

She liked going to parties; it was better than the garden and the Women's Institute. If she got bored she would go home early and get someone else to see me home. One time at a dance given by a Liberal peer she got very sleepy and bored and decided to go upstairs to one of the bedrooms and have a bit of a kip. I hadn't realized this and Francis and I happened to go into the room and there was Mama fast asleep in the middle of the bed.

People made a fuss about so many things. I remember that one girl was living with a man whom she was not married to and her mother gave a dinner before a dance in his flat. My mother made a great kerfuffle about my going, but I was longing to see what sin was like. I could not believe that anyone could be so dowdy and so sinful.

I had lovely clothes because I knew a *vendeuse* at Paquin, and while I was in France I had lodged with people who knew Paul Poiret's sister. The first dance I ever went to I wore a Paul Poiret dress with very tight sleeves and I was so nervous I could not get my soup spoon to my mouth. It was a very beautiful dress with two trains but later I got one of them in the lavatory pan. I had an absolute up-and-downer with my mother over my coming-out dress. She wanted it to be white but I had it in pale pink organza. She thought the front was too low.

I shared a dance in April with two girls, one of whom we did not like very much. The other was not terribly successful because she could not see the point. She is a marvellous-looking woman but she preferred to sit and watch people. We had it at 23 Knightsbridge which was one of the places Searcy's owned, where Agriculture House is now.

The young men who did the season were so unutterably stupid you could not believe it. But you see, anyone who was doing anything interesting did not bother to do it. The young men were either army or just very dull and old-fashioned. I can see now how stupid most of the regulars were. You should see the ones who were the successful debs today. By and large, the ones who were the successful debs— and they were not necessarily the beautiful ones—were the ones who made a lot of noise. There was always a sub-conscious divide between the upper-class deb and the middle-class one, who usually tried harder. They knew all the catch phrases— "isn't it amusing, my dear?"—and they did the Lambeth Walk. Now they are all rather fat crippled old ladies with jerseys drooping around the edge. The really beautiful ones were not necessarily a great success, either because they were not terribly interested or because they had enough self-assurance not to bother. There were, of course, the professionals like Lady St John of Bletso and Lady

Clancarty; we called her Lady Blank Cartridge. It was all terribly discreet and they usually brought out poor little rich girls or perhaps the daughters of widowers or South African magnates. Whether or not they had a successful season really depended on what they were like, but they did seem to be rather plain girls. But maybe that was because they were not having a nice time which does seem to affect your looks at that age.

All the "deb's delights" knew all the catch-phrases. But it was often all rather shabby genteel, except at some of the grand parties like those at Belvoir. I think the best picture is the one Anthony Powell gives in his description of the Walpole-Wilsons, slightly unchic, with always a lot of people around in that ghastly house with the picture in the hall. Do you know, there was no such thing as a dinner dress—so that, at least if you were people like the Walpole-Wilsons, you wore your last year's evening dresses.

I came out in 1937 so I was presented to George VI. I went with my sister, who spent all her time looking at the pictures. She was very clever because she knew where to go so that we could see things. You went round and round rather like musical chairs and had to stop wherever you happened to be. My sisters were much older than me and they had done the season in the "roaring twenties" when it was much less formal, and just a few dances with a gramophone. That was before it started to get grand again.

I went to Ascot with my sister, who was sixteen years older than I was. I quite enjoyed it because although I don't like racing it was a chance to see people other than those of your own age. My sister told me that I must be very careful and that perhaps someone would offer us tea, but if they didn't I must be sure to eat as much as possible because it was very expensive. No one did offer us tea, so in the end we went into a tent where there were people like the Duke of Norfolk and Noel Coward and I thought it strange that no one had offered them tea. So I ate a lot and then my sister tried to pay. I saw her going a bit white because the attendant said, "There is no charge, Miss, this is the Jockey Club".

I didn't go to nightclubs much because they were too expensive. Francis did not want to go and he didn't have the dough. I never went to the Embassy but I do remember going to the Coconut Grove. We had been to a frightfully dull party in Essex near where my mother lived and four of us decided to go to London. But we only had a frightful old banger so we went to my mother's house to pick up her car and came back a couple of hours later. In the morning, when I came downstairs I could hear my mother saying to a policeman, "But it's impossible. The car has been in the garage all night." What had happened was that it had been used for a smash and grab raid while we were in the Coconut Grove, and then put back, with the rugs folded just as they had been so we noticed nothing. Fortunately my Mama was not too cross because she thought it made a good story.

I did enjoy some of the dances, especially if Francis or my particular chums were there, and if they were held in interesting houses. I remember one marvellous one held in the derelict house Maud Allen owned in Regent's Park. It was taken by Mrs Phillipson, who had really launched Syrie Maugham. She was bringing out her two nieces, the Dunns. It was dreamy. The house was quite derelict, and butter muslin had been placed over all the walls with great wall vases full of cow parsley.

None of the grass had been cut so you could just wander out onto the long grass. Mr Physick from Searcy's told my mother that 120 chickens had gone into the soup and she was really quite shocked. I think for the first time she became aware of the cost and wastefulness which had not occurred to her before. But it was a lovely, lovely evening.

I did gain quite a lot from the season. I made one or two very good friends. Because of Francis I never felt personally very involved, but I was able to sit back and observe. I did not get married till just before the war started because he was only earning £150 a year and my mother wanted us to wait, although she did say we could marry if war became definite. So we married the day after Hitler invaded Poland.

If I had had a daughter, I would not have brought her out—anyway, I do not think she would have wanted to do it because she would have heard it being debunked so much. One of my two sons refused to go to anything at all. The other would only go if a dance was being held somewhere pretty like Syon Park. I was asked to a couple of luncheon parties and I thought because I had two sons I would be the belle of the luncheon, but as soon as the mothers discovered I did not have a daughter they were not interested. It was so narrow. They were simply concerned with getting invitations for their daughters.'

In 1938, girls were still being sent off to finishing schools in Paris. 'They were fearfully expensive by today's values,' one recalls, '£120 a term. I had resisted the whole thing but my mother wanted me to do everything that was socially right and proper. I got caught up with some very snobby girls who were horrified later to find me working in Peter Jones. There were nine of us at the school. We learnt bridge, we did a cathedral a week and a museum a week. Wherever we went we were escorted. If you went to the hairdresser, someone sat there to make sure you weren't assaulted or something. I found it very difficult because I had been fairly free in London. The Russian who taught us bridge had taught the Spanish royal family and constantly went on about *"mes enfants d'Espagne."* We always had biscuits and lemonade while we had our bridge lessons. We went to the opera but we had to leave before the last act of Faust because the ending was not considered suitable.'

Lady Sibell confided in the May *Harpers' Bazaar*, 'Debutantes are particularly gay and pretty this year. Entertaining is being done in a big way, heralded by the large ball given by Lady Moncrieffe at Dudley House for her daughter Elizabeth. At the March and April balls, oyster bars supplanted last year's beer garden. Chaperons banned the "Big Apple", also the "Palais Glide". Chaperons danced a good deal more; the popular Viennese waltzes bring them all out and the bridge tables are deserted. Debutantes are still forbidden to pop off to nightclubs; dining alone or going to the cinema with a best beau is frowned on. Favourite dance tunes are "Nice Work if You Can Get It", "Remember Me", "Popcorn Man", and "A Foggy Day".

This was, in *Harpers'* view, very much the Queen's year. Next May, George VI and Elizabeth went on an official visit to Canada and the United States, only returning to England at the end of June. *Harpers'* reported that cheers resounded from across the Atlantic from the triumphal royal progress, and that, in England, the royal duchesses piloted the social world with charm and skill. But it was becoming impossible to ignore events in Europe, and politics dominated all conversation.

4

BELOW STAIRS

*B*ehind all the social eventing was a back-up force of servants and trades-men whose livelihood depended on the existence of the upper classes and the diary of the season. In 1921 there were 1,209,704 domestic servants in the country. The Depression led to an increase, with numbers rising again, so that by 1931 there were 1,410,713. In London alone, in 1921, the 181,980 domestic servants accounted for 14.8 per cent of the work-force. It was never the same after the Second World War—even in the 1930s, the middle classes were turning to the 'char': by 1931 there were 140,146, where there had been 118,476 in 1921—although some of the very grand families had remarkably large staffs even in the 1950s. But just as the season had returned to its former splendour, at least superficially, after the Great War, so the servants took off their khaki and went back.

Servants were a basic fact of life. Etiquette books always included chapters on how to deal with them. 'In all cases,' wrote Lady Troubridge in her *Book of Etiquette*, first published in 1926 but frequently reprinted right up till the end of the 1940s, 'when parties are given in the country, arrangements should be made for stabling horses, parking cars and feeding the servants . . . to arrange a buffet for tea, bread and butter and cake for visiting servants, is neither expensive or difficult and certainly should be done.'

The doyen of the servants was the butler, very much lord of his own patch, but the lady's maid held a position of supreme importance; she was essential for the debutante, putting out her clothes, packing for her, accompanying her on weekends sometimes chaperoning her. Her duties were defined by Lady Troubridge as follows: 'The maid has the care of her mistress's wardrobe and jewellery, and toilet-table. She writes notes to the dressmaker and such persons, does her mistress's shopping when required, packs and unpacks, and waits on her mistress. She does not do any housework, though by special arrangement she may undertake the care of the linen closet, do the flowers, and, perhaps, dust her mistress's bedroom. The maid should be an educated, superior person, and is addressed as Miss or Mrs So-and-so by the other servants. She expects a workroom, or a bedroom and workroom combined, and she is not required to do her own room.' Lady's maids, she goes on, 'when travelling with their ladies, wear neat coats and skirts and neat quiet hats.'

Rosina Harrison, who became lady's maid to Nancy, Lady Astor, was originally maid to her daughter Phyllis ('Miss Wissie'). Rose Harrison came from a Yorkshire family and she and her two sisters all went into service, although only Rose reached the height of being a lady's maid. Now retired, the three share a house, divided into flats, in Worthing.

*Page 50: Behind Cecil Beaton's photograph of Nancy,
Lady Astor, is a detail of Fragonard's* The Swing: *but
behind every deb and hostess of the 1930s was a large
back-up staff of butlers, ladies' maids, and other
servants. In their own way, many of the staff enjoyed
the travels and dinners that were part of the debs'
season.*

As lady's maid, Rose had definitely reached the higher echelons, whereas Ann was a housemaid and Olive a cook. The kitchen staff were a world apart from the lady's maids, who were often considered snobs. As Olive remembers:

'Lady's maids were always on about society. They were never popular. They were almost as bad as the nannies, and I wouldn't work in a house where there was a nursery. Nanny would always be coming in to say "Johnny wants this" and "Little Alice won't eat that". I remember I was in one house, with Mrs Faith Moore, and the maid Miss Bromley was a real snob. I was first kitchen maid and if the cook went out, she'd say to me, "Look after Miss Bromley, see she has everything," and they did want a lot because they tried to ape the lady. But Miss Bromley discovered that I had a sister who was a lady's maid, and it all changed; she would often come and have a cup of tea with me. But she didn't bother to get on with the rest of the staff.'

The lady's maid travelled with her mistress so that her shifts from town to country depended on the season. As Lady Astor's maid, Rose Harrison was constantly on the move. The Astors had five houses, including 4 St James's Square and Cliveden; there were journeys down to the constituency in Plymouth as well as weekending and moves for the racing calendar. 'We went all over the place. There was so much packing with Lady Astor. Once when she went to Ascot, I had to take 46 hats and all the outfits and she only went on Ladies' Day. It was no sooner packed and unpacked than it was time to pack again. I used to say they knew their own way into the packing cases.'

But at first she was Miss Wissie's maid, and as such had gone with her to America for the season there. 'Lady Astor took us over but I stayed there with her, with her aunt. I went to the balls with her. I had to stay till one, two, or three in the morning. But I was allowed to stay in bed in the morning and have breakfast there.'

Back in England, Miss Wissie was of course presented:

'The actual presentation was like getting ready for the Coronation. Lady Astor was always going to court at that time. She presented various American ladies and her own nieces. They'd wear beautiful plain dresses with a train at the back and three feathers on a silk net. They all wore tiaras—Lady Astor had five. Lady Astor had a great feather fan, but I think Miss Wissie carried a purse. And they had beautiful cloaks lined in sable or ermine. And they always went to the state balls at Buckingham Palace. I never went, but Mr Lee, our butler, knew the house-keeper at Buckingham Palace and he had seen one.

Girls were chaperoned everywhere and never allowed to go out alone. They never went out with girl-friends, always with elder relations, sisters or married cousins. No one resented it; certainly Miss Wissie never questioned it. Mothers trusted you. They'd write to you and say, "I know you'll do your utmost to see my daughter is smart".

Lady Violet Astor gave a dance for Miss Wissie at Hever Castle, a big party for her. I saw Lady Astor at Cliveden and she said Miss Wissie was to wear a certain dress. When I told Miss Wissie, she didn't want to wear it. I didn't want to be at the centre of a row, so I asked Miss Wissie what she wanted to wear and she said a lovely gold dress she had. So I got that out for her and dressed her up that night, and off she went to the ball. We stayed that night and went back to Cliveden the next afternoon. Lady Astor sent for me and said, "Rose, I hear Miss Wissie was the belle of the ball". "How nice," I said. Now Lady Astor was always very critical, but this time she said how well everything had gone, so when everything was in my favour and there were no complaints, I told her ladyship that Miss Wissie hadn't worn the dress her ladyship had wanted. But by then Lady Astor couldn't really say anything. There were no more complaints and Miss Wissie and I just went on.

As lady's maid, you had to put out the clothes and prepare the bath. I would put out all the linen and perhaps lay out two dresses. I never went into the bathroom of any of my ladies. Miss Wissie had a big bedroom with a bathroom off it and she would call me once she was dressed, and I would fasten her clothes and perhaps put her pearls on. But she did her own hair; I never touched hair. She had thick straight hair. I prepared a purse if she was going out to dinner. I would get her an evening cloak, often one of her mother's. Lady Astor chose all her daughter's clothes. She had so many, but Miss Wissie didn't bother so much. I didn't sit up at night for her if I hadn't gone with her. I would put her clothes away in the morning. It was only when her ladyship got old that I ever sat up. I preferred to, so that I could put her jewels in the safe. I couldn't sleep if I didn't do that.

But sometimes I would take Miss Wissie to a ball. We'd go to the cloakroom to see everything was in order and then I'd give her into the charge of the lady who was giving the ball. Then you'd finished with her till it was time to go home. Sometimes I might take a book and sometimes I would talk to all the maids that I knew. It would only be from about ten till one usually. We'd gossip and have sandwiches and coffee. If it was a late ball, we had eggs and bacon at four or five in the morning just as they did. If it was big dinner, they'd all wear their medals. I've never seen anyone with more medals than Lady Cromer. But the smartest lady was Marchioness Curzon of Kedlestone. She and Lady Alexandra Metcalfe, the wife of Fruity Metcalfe, always looked as if they'd come out of bandboxes. Margaret Sweeny was beautiful, and the Duchess of Buccleuch, and Mollie Lascelles when she had her tiara on. There was nothing out of place and they carried themselves well. They behaved like ladies. They kept their place and we kept ours. Those days were so beautiful. Even the food was beautiful: there were French chefs, Austrian chefs.

It was a life of variety. There were tennis parties and weekend parties. We went to the hunt balls, we went to Scotland, to so many places I can't remember them all. It was a nice life; this was 1928/9. I always had a nice room. I had tea in the morning in my bedroom and a fire in the room. The housekeeper would show us over the house at lunchtime when everyone had gone hunting. Later on, I used to do the same myself. I was better off in those days than I am now.

The houses were full of flowers; there were always twenty or thirty gardeners. The asparagus came from the garden; the fruit came from the garden. There was the still-room, where all the jams were made and the cakes and breakfast-rolls—the trays went from there in the morning, then into the kitchen and up to the ladies.

The maids' life was in the steward's room; there was the butler and house-keeper, the lady's maid and any visiting maids and valets. There was a tremendous atmosphere, but no jealousy. It was a hard life but everyone knew their place. The housekeeper was in charge of the housemaids. She looked after the fruit for the dining table and she was responsible for the china, the Spode and the Dresden, and the coffee cups. The dining table was always marvellous, but that was under the supervision of the butler. Footmen would wait at table and after that there might be music and a little dancing.

I never wore a uniform; just something quiet and neat, navy blue or black, sometimes brown. Lots of lady's maids got clothes given to them, but Lady Astor was tiny and Miss Wissie was very tall and slim, so it was no good for me, though Lady Astor did give me some beautiful jewellery—I had to sell it when I bought a bungalow to put my mother in.

I didn't want to marry because I enjoyed my job and I liked travelling with them. You'd meet, say, the lady's maid of the Duchess of Portland and then you might find yourself staying there with a party of young people. Wages weren't up to scratch by today's standards, and I didn't get anything extra for clothes. I would buy one outfit which lasted the year—it had to. But I did get one fur-lined coat from Lady Astor. I still have it. She said to me, "Rose, I'm going to give that coat away," and I said, "Well, you can give it to me, your ladyship". She told me she'd never seen me looking so pleased.

Now I'm with my two sisters; we're the Three Graces, three sisters in service. But it's different now. When I was in service, I wasn't used to cooking and clean-ing. But then the rich were rich and the poor were poor. Ask my sister—poor little scullery maids, their hands were often red-raw.'
Olive backs her up:

'I started in the scullery when there were four in the kitchen and the scullery maid had to do all the hard work—washing up, cleaning the copper with silver sand and vinegar. You worked your way up. The vegetable maid did the vegetables for the dining room and the staff. The second kitchen maid did the garnishes and

cooked for the staff. The first kitchen maid did the sweet and fish course and helped the cook. It was totally different to being a lady's maid. They were waited on, but often you'd see the kitchen maids crying. They might not finish washing up after lunch till four, and then they had to start preparing vegetables for dinner. And it was one afternoon off a week, from four to ten, so there was no time to do anything.

If there was a really formal dinner, there would be one chef for each course. One for the soup with a maid to do the garnishes; one for the fish, and another for the meat; one for the sweet course and helping with the sugar work; and one for the savouries. If royalty came, there'd be *petits fours*, all made in the kitchen, baskets of fruit—I took one home to mother once and she could't believe it was sugar and kept it till it crumbled away—and another time there was a beehive covered in bees.'

'London was full of servants,' says Rose, 'there was Crewe House—that was the Duke of Roxburgh's—Sutherland House, Londonderry House, Lansdowne—now that's a club. Perhaps the most beautiful of all was Holland House. That burned down during the war. In those days if you had no money you had to go into service. You never answered an advertisement; you always went to an agency. I got jobs in London and then I lowered my sisters down to join me.'

The third sister, Ann, became a housemaid. 'I worked my way up. I landed one job where the lady was very erratic and counted the linen, so I walked round the corner in my print frock and got a job looking after six bachelor flats. In service, we had to go round after the gentlemen had had baths and polish the soap so it looked as if it hadn't been used.'

At that time, they conclude, they had to work hard, but the system worked. 'The Astors,' Rose points out, 'had eleven cars and five chauffeurs—a lot of staff. In the same way, the season was useful because it created work and the mothers could stay at home and know that their daughters were well looked after. We were like detectives, really, but that was the way life was lived. After the war, there were only the garden parties and now they are not even presented. It is obsolete, but now everything has gone down. It was a grand life really, I liked it. It was hard labour for some, but I was spoilt and I got used to living nicely. The debutantes enjoyed themselves. They married within their class—not like now, when they marry commoners and the next thing you read there is a divorce. It was a different era, a different life.'

In her retirement, Rose has started writing books, something she had always wanted to do. Her first, about her life with Lady Astor, was a best-seller, and she followed it by *Gentlemen's Gentlemen*, interviewing the butlers and footmen she had known and worked with. Their attitude is very similar to hers—that it was a hard life, but interesting with good perks. They would travel with their employers, first class, across the Atlantic. They had positions of real authority, and in their own world below stairs they received great respect. Gordon Grimmett, who also worked with the Astors, told her, 'When I look back to the day I left school, I was a country lout, nothing more. It was from the moment that I went into service that my education began . . . . You learn to distinguish what is good and what is not, you look at books lining shelves and eventually you pick one up and begin to read.'

A typical day for Gordon Grimmett was like this:

'Every morning would see us up at seven, running down to the still-room, eventually emerging with six small morning tea-trays arranged on one large butler's tray, distributing them round the guests' rooms, opening the curtains and gently but firmly waking them. We didn't want to have them slipping off to sleep again and blaming us for having missed breakfast. Then collecting their clothes from the night before, whipping them into the brushing room, sponging, brushing, folding and hanging them. Then laying the breakfast table, and bringing in the various dishes—kidneys, bacon, eggs, fish on one side of the dining room; hams, brawns and galantines and game pies on the other. And the constant running to and fro with fresh toast and hot rolls.

After breakfast came the cleaning of silver, then hall duties; at St James's Square, the duty footman would be stationed all day sitting in a large hooded leather chair. . . . Then there was the running and taking of messages. We were permanently busy. And then lunch.'

At the Astors' this was always pandemonium, with numbers going up all the time and footmen having to add extra leaves to the dining table. Dinners were, of course, more formal; full dress and decorations would be worn, except by some Labour MPs who had principles about not dressing up.

Edwin Lee was the Astors' butler, and he describes Mr Will Thorn's arrival at one reception:

'It is one thing having principles and another living up to them, as Mr Thorn was to find out. He came on foot to St James's Square, and seeing the dazzling array of guests in full dress with their ladies in mink and tiaras, he took fright. He decided to linger around until most of the guests had arrived. He didn't do it for long because he was apprehended by a police officer, who wanted to charge him with loitering with intent. He was able to talk his way out of that, but it hadn't done his self-confidence any good, so he decided to enter. Gordon Grimmett was the footman on duty . . . and had to inform me of the identity of each guest. I'd just announced a distinguished member of the peerage with a string of decorations and appointments, when up piped Gordon with, "Mr William Thorn," then dropping to a stage whisper he continued, "turned-down collar, coloured shirt and tie, blue suit, cut-away short jacket." I managed to get Mr Thorn's name out and to signal to the announcer to continue his duties before I fled upstairs howling with laughter.'

After the war, there were still houses which kept large staff, but too often, complains Peter Whiteley, who entered service just after the war, the servants were untrained or half-trained: 'Many of them were foreign and unused to our way. . . . If they were experienced, they were old, and trying to run a house with old retainers is neither exciting or rewarding, particularly when employers expected the old standards.'

Attitudes and expectations had both changed. The standard of living was rising; people preferred to take other work, and other work was available. The very rich would still have servants, but never again on the scale of pre-war years.

5

DOING THEIR BIT

O n Sunday, 3 September 1939, the inevitable happened and war was declared. Yet despite the preceding months of crises, people were still taken unawares. Searcy's order-book was full and cocktail parties and dances had to be cancelled. Large numbers of people were on holiday abroad.

The society glossies like *Harpers'*, with longish printing schedules, were slow to reflect events and the September issue carried the new Paris fashions. Gradually the mood of the papers changed. Society events became less important and patriotism came to the fore. People were encouraged to keep up morale. If ladies were writing to friends abroad, they were enjoined not to mention the bombing but to do a bit of sales talk for Britain and encourage their friends to buy British goods.

The *Tatler* was able to respond more quickly to events and in the light of the Nazi-Soviet pact in August, pictured racing at York with the comment that it should be headed 'A Study in Imperturbability'. In its 6 September issue it reported that the 'crisis robbed Deauville of many of its most regular supporters before Grand Prix days,' yet 'there was still a good attendance for a very exciting day's racing'.

By its 13 September edition, which had the King's message to the nation as its frontispiece, there was a spate of weddings, often with the groom in uniform—marriages, it said, 'that have been hurried up by the current spot of bother'. Already, Hector Powe were starting to advertise 'Uniforms for Women' for the three services. Cyclax named their new lipstick 'Auxiliary Red'—aiming this new colour firmly at the service woman.

A week later, its social news concentrated on the plight of the British trying to get home: 'Amid the discomforts of travel during the General Mobilization in France, hardships are outweighed for ordinary travellers by the dramatic interest of the circumstances. . . . Captain and Mrs George Troyte-Bullock (lovely Nina Rathbone) took days and days from the Dalmatian coast and nearly had to go round by Greece, but finally travelled the length of Italy's boot hearing everywhere the same rumours of *Il Duce*'s poor health . . .'.

Everybody seems to have behaved frightfully well: 'Biarritzois, like most people, were a little caught off-balance at the last moment by the high speed with which things rushed to the unfortunate climax, but equally, like everywhere else, they preserved an admirable composure.'

The *Tatler* praised the Queen for hitting 'a happy medium in the clothes she is wearing; not too bright and painfully *chic*, nor dreary and unfeminine. Women who make the war an excuse to wear their shabbiest blacks, unrelieved by even a clean white collar, are asking to be run over. . . . The small proportion of Mayfair which has not gone to the country (Mrs Charles Sweeny is rolling bandages) has got an attack of "uniformitis" with blacks as the only alternative.'

From this time on, uniforms predominated, the only racing was in 'peaceful Eire' and sometimes there were parties photographed in America. 'Instead of sleek limousines, the Savoy Hotel Garage now holds lorries converted into ambulances, and those who once went along to the Grill for lunch now have their meals brought to the garage.' Rolls-Royce and Bentley soon had to take advertisements announcing they were temporarily ceasing to manufacture motor-car chassis at the request of the government. From Paris, Priscilla wrote in her newsletter, 'As I feared, my domestic staff, after having stood the mobilisation like stoics, jibbed badly when war was actually declared.' They had to be packed off to the country whereas Priscilla, to give her her due, does seem to have survived the whole war in Paris with some fortitude.

It was not all gloom in London. In October, *Tatler* had a page of photographs entitled 'Behind London's Black-Out', with the encouraging caption, 'Though London's streets are still black, restaurants and the places where they dance are (behind light traps reminiscent of the older sort of nightclub) turning up their lights to shine "o'er fair women and brave men". The main change from pre-war days is sartorial; uniforms and the lounge suits of the civil defence workers (with uniforms of khaki and navy and air-force blue predominant) having invaded the strongholds of the white tie. Quaglino's and the Café de Paris were among the first to adjust themselves to war conditions and are now nightly gathering to themselves people temporarily "off-parade".'

Harpers' confirmed this in January 1940 with their piece 'PM AM': 'London restaurants are all jampacked. It is necessary to book a table even if escorted by an admiral, general or air marshal. The Berkeley has the *place d'honneur* as it had in the last war. The Coq d'Or cuisine continues famous, Prunier's especially for lunch on Sundays, Quaglino's the favourite rendezvous for Sunday evening, the cocktail dance at the Berkeley for the 5 to 7 period. The Savoy is heavily patronised by the Navy and diplomats, the Ivy by the stage. The Ritz has the smartest snack bar.' It went on to advise, 'For the best four-o'clock-in-the-morning dive ask your taxi driver.'

The social team on the *Tatler* even claimed that they had found the exigencies of war some relief. In April, the 'And the World Said' column read, 'This department, having spent Easter in London for the first time in ten years, wishes to record its personal gratitude to the Fuhrer for temporarily removing Le Touquet from the map of England. If there was one thing about collecting social bits which bored us more

By 1945 Germany had surrendered, and the Marchioness of Tavistock's picnic for the Eton/Harrow Match that year was held in a more relaxed atmosphere.

than another, it was standing in the cold blast by the first tee, listening to stock-brokers ask each other what time they went to bed. . . . This Easter, the Right People were scattered, though many stayed in London where the Ritz provided a first-tee bench for Lady Pamela Berry (cornflowers on her black coat) and the Duchess of Westminster (green and blue ribbons dropping from the back of her hat) . . .'.

The *Tatler* encouraged the reader later in May by the thought that restaurants still flourished, as they had in Madrid during the Civil War. 'The immediate effect of total war on the restaurant world was dampening [but] people must eat, and most people like to talk and gape between mouthfuls, whatever happens. At Claridge's, the magnificence of the air-raid shelter and its vaunted powers of resistance induce a temporary glow of well-being. So does an extraordinary liqueur in the Causerie called "Cloc Cacao". . . Claridge's is the diplomats' automat.'

Soon they were giving practical suggestions on what to wear in the air-raid shelter and congratulating Marshall and Snelgrove for coming up with a suitable hat, 'felt reinforced with a lightweight steel cap . . . fitted with rubber round the edge to prevent undue pressure.' According to *Tatler*, 'Many women in emergencies like to wear a hat, as it gives them a sense of proportion.' *Harpers'* in November the same year admitted that slacks had become an unofficial uniform and hinted that 'if your work chips your varnish terribly, you may have to give it up altogether' (nicely ambiguous). It suggested a special gas mask holder: 'Elizabeth Arden makes cases in velvet, all shades, with a silk lined pocket fitted up with beauty preparations on top; also in waterproof satin and in waterproofed snow-leopard velvet—very good in a blackout'. The same issue boasted it still carried over 20 pages of advertising and pointed out proudly that its fashion shots were taken during air raid alerts, so there, Goebbels! 'The Smart Englishwoman of the Blitz,' it went on, with photographs to make the point, 'is perfectly dressed because she has simple standards she keeps even after a night in a stuffy shelter.'

For the rest of the war, the reader was being constantly encouraged by photographs of society ladies, young and old, engaged in war work of various kinds—Lady Sarah Spencer-Churchill, for example, doing factory work, or Lady Courtney, wife of Air Marshal Sir Charles Courtney, working for the London County Council Fire Station, Knightsbridge Branch; 'some of her friends are giving cocktail parties at which collections are made'. In 1943, readers learned that Lady Tavistock 'manages without a "Nannie" and looks after Robin entirely by herself. Her fresh and feminine blouses are contrived from a long-treasured collection of old lace.'

But as the *Tatler* wrote in May 1940, 'Debutante is a word with a hollow ring to it this year with the war clamping down on the Courts and the usual functions of a London Season, but there are many beautiful girls coming out in the quieter fashion appropriate to the time.' The only regular social event to continue throughout the war, although in an altered form, was the Queen Charlotte's Hospital Ball. This ball had been revived as a charity dance in 1925 as a means of raising money for Chelsea Hospital for Women, and named after the wife of George III, who on her birthday liked to be surrounded by her family and Maids of Honour and to have her cake brought in to the music of Handel's *Judas Maccabeus*. In the 1920s and 1930s it was just one of a number of charity functions that a debutante might attend, but its survival during the war years gave it a more important place. It was recognized as being a deb's unofficial coming-out, in the absence of the courts, a position it maintained even when presentations revived. During the war the proceeds went to various service charities. Often more than one ball was held, partly because it was no longer held in the very large ballroom at Grosvenor House.

Bill Saville started playing at Queen Charlotte's in 1942, when he was in the RAF, and his orchestra went on providing the music up till 1972. 'Then,' he remembers, 'it was a semi-service job. We started in the big ballroom downstairs but then the Americans took that over and we had to have it in two halves in the other ballroom.' Even in the war years it made a good profit. In 1944, when tickets were £3 and people had to bring their own food and drink, 1,300 tickets were sold and they made £2,482 clear. But for the wartime deb there was little else; as the *Tatler* put it, 'Their "Season" is war work'.

6

RATIONING AND RECOVERY

*I*t was only gradually that the season revived in the post-war years. In their eagerness, the magazines slightly anticipated its full burgeoning, which did not occur till the very end of the decade. *Harpers' Bazaar* enthused, 'Summer 1945, it's the biggest coming-out season there's ever been. Whether you're seventeen or twenty-two, this is the magic year of your life.' The *Queen* in May 1945 was equally optimistic, although it did add a cautious rider. The King and Queen, it reported, were to hold garden parties. 'Several thousand invitation cards will be sent out for each occasion but the parties will have the same informality which marked the occasional little gathering held at Windsor during the war. It is probable that debutantes who missed coming out in the past six years and older women who have similarly been unable to attend a Royal Court, will have the opportunity of being presented at special garden parties. There is a lengthy list of such presentations however. It may take two years to get through them all. I understand it is probable that the Royal Courts will not be held until after the end of the war with Japan.'

In many ways, it was astonishing that the season revived at all. There had been six years of war, the atom bomb had been dropped, the Labour party had come to power and under Attlee a minor social revolution had begun. Britain was struggling through days of shortages, grimmer than any years of the war, with rationing, coupons, power cuts and finally the bitter winter of 1946/7 which did little to encourage the royal family to return to the formalities of an exclusive circle. Yet it did revive— modified a little, and with perhaps more emphasis on cash than breeding.

In fact, it was not until 1947 that presentations began again. By then, more than 20,000 people were waiting to apply. This was far too great a number for the formality of the pre-war evening courts, when each debutante and her sponsor were personally presented. Instead, the presentations took the form of garden parties and attendance alone counted as presentation. Appalling weather in 1948 led to the parties being transferred to the State Apartments and this was the routine until 1951. The rules for dress naturally changed. They were now 'Ladies: Day Dress with Hat. Gentlemen: Morning Dress or Uniform or Lounge Suit.' At these parties, only the ladies of the Diplomatic Corps, exercising their traditional right, were actually presented, making their curtsey to the King and Queen in the ballroom. The other guests filled the State Apartments, and after the diplomatic presentations the King and Queen circulated, speaking to individuals.

The *Queen* decided that the advent of the garden party was a great success, solving the presentation problem. 'Because no Courts were held during the war, there are now eight times as many applicants for presentation as there were in 1939.' Even the death of the Earl of Harewood, the husband of Princess Mary, failed to put a damper on proceedings.

Once the seal of royal approval had been set, there was little, apart from the difficulties of catering, to deter the diehard or the ambitious from perpetuating the season. It was true that there was no party for Princess Margaret; her seventeenth birthday, the *Queen* reported in September 1947, which was celebrated quietly, was to be regarded as her coming out. 'The prettiest Princess in Europe,' it went on, 'will be abandoning her studies in French, at which she is the Royal Family expert, geography, history and, alas, the piano (a promising pupil).' But carefully arranged dinners before coming-out parties, luncheon parties and debs' tea parties came back, even if the rigidity of the 1930s had gone.

So how were they catered for? Authoress Barbara Fontannaz recalls the pigeon casseroles, venison and game; the rum and orange, Service gin and lime—but always excellent champagne. Hostesses produced dinner for twelve or luncheons for twenty with bartered sugar and black-market eggs, while guests arrived with their individual —pats of butter and slices of wholemeal bread. There were sumptuous looking puddings which tasted of nothing, mayonnaisse helped out with liquid paraffin, strawberries without cream. Even the debutante cake at Queen Charlotte's Ball had to be a mixture of dried eggs and currants, while rebels were beginning to say 'I will not curtsey to a cake'.

They were dread, dull, drear difficult years and yet there were glamorous debutantes like Raine McCorquodale who married Viscount Lewisham, the heir to the Earl of Dartmouth, at the end of her season. And there was, of course, a royal wedding. The engagement of Princess Elizabeth to Prince Philip was announced at midnight on 9 July 1947. That night she had attended a ball given at Apsley House, which the Duke of Wellington had lent to his niece Lady Serena James. Tommy Kinsman and his band played, and Tommy Kinsman thereupon became the debs' band-leader, a position he maintained till the end of the 1950s:

'I suddenly got really established. Before that I didn't have much money. I used to go down to relieve a band which played at a hotel near Sevenoaks. We went once a week on their night off, and I would get 30 bob for playing and another 30 bob for driving the band down. Then Lady Serena James asked me to play for her dance at Apsley House—you know, Number One, London—which her uncle was lending to her. I was booked the night she wanted me and so I said to her could it be the night after. It was the best thing I could have done. All that day there were rumours that Princess Elizabeth was going to get engaged and she was at the party. Crowds gathered, as they will in London, and at midnight her engagement was announced. We all got so much publicity and after that, everybody wanted to book us.

The girls used to tell my drummer, "Oh, I'm in love with Tommy". But I was never a menace with the girls. I treated them all with the same respect and I never made a date with a girl I was working for. They used to bring me mascots, little dogs and dolls and flowers. But I respected the people I worked for and I always felt that if I did get mixed up with one of them, there would be jealousy among the others and I might lose some of my work.

At that stage, there were all kinds of things on the ration, like petrol. There was a limited price for meals, even at places like Claridge's and the Savoy. It was all shepherd's pie, or chicken if you got there early enough.

I always knew who was going to dance with Princess Elizabeth, because they used to come up to me—this included Prince Philip himself—and try to bribe me not to play anything too hectic. They wanted something nice and light, something easy. But they all liked nice, easy dances. I think that was part of the reason for my band's success; if we played a quick-step, I used to take it at a slower speed, a nice, easy tempo, so that it was just one foot in front of the other. We used to call it "tired businessman's tempo".'

The New Look, Barbara Fontannaz remembers, had mothers stretching their ingenuity. But debutantes could be seen in the pages of the *Tatler* wearing dresses made from mattress ticking, upholstery fabrics, stiffened muslin acquired in finishing schools in Switzerland, and brocades smuggled in from Dublin, which welcomed the chance to champion another lost cause. 'Secondhand shops,' she goes on, 'in Mayfair and Knightsbridge sold old clothes with exclusive labels and some mothers dabbled in black markets. Setting a scene of unparalleled ugliness, the forties produced skimpy dresses with puffed sleeves, boned bodices and heart-shaped necklines. There were also peep-toed shoes, fur muffs and a great many ancient cock feathers better not displayed. Attics disgorged grannies' furs and their ancestors' lace fichus and crinolines and, if the New Look heralded the return of the feminine and the romantic (11 inches from the ground), it hung itself with yards of lace and velvet tacked on to standard clothing. Nobody had enough coupons to refurbish an austerity wardrobe.'

These years, she thinks, ensured the success of the Highland balls, the last bastion of the gentry:

'Confidence was restored to a despondent catering trade and hotels, restaurants and nightclubs swayed with love and old lace. It was no cause for surprise. Price controls suited the young men now returning to Oxford and Cambridge whose Commem and May balls were part of the season. In any case, what young officer could cavil at a 5s-plus-dinner dance, especially when accompanied by live bands whose individual leaders serenaded each publicized lady with her favourite tune? On the evenings when there were no coming-out dances, everyone flocked to see their chosen band leader—Edmundo Ross at the Bagatelle, Carol Gibbons at the Savoy, Chappie d'Amato at Hatchett's, Marlene and Coward at the Café de Paris.

There may have been hints of a laxity in morals—the equerries may have quipped that the season is more like a brothel than a marriage mart—but there were still the nice girls who danced with the godfathers, brothers and friends of older sisters. These were the girls who never visited a man's room alone or went unchaperoned to a house party. Between them, these nice girls, with their Kensington voices and hand-me-downs, compiled their own list of who or what was desirable, passing on a code: M.T.F.—must touch flesh; N.S.T.—not safe in taxis, or M.S.C.—makes skin creep.

But during the 1940s it was fashionable to attend, for the first time, at least three debutante dances on the same evening, thereby disrupting a hostess's carefully arranged dinner set and, for the first time, men gate-crashed dances for free suppers and debutantes were seen at nightclubs.'

Barbara Fontannaz considers that already, because of these changes, the writing was on the wall for the season, but she admits it must have been healthy because it did take such a long time to die. Certainly by 1949, when the parties were really getting going again, things seemed much as they had always been. Clothes came off the ration that March, although the meat ration was again reduced. This was the year that Sallyann Vivian, a cousin of the Marquess of Bath and now Mrs Charles Wilson, made her debut. Fair-haired, with a 20-inch waist (as the press continually commented), she was dubbed Debutante of the Year:

'I really enjoyed it. It was all great fun. The parties were lovely and I don't remember anyone worrying about rationing. Because of the war I had been to boarding school in the country, whereas before I had lived in London and had a governess. There were a set of children whose nannies took them to the park, so I did know a lot of girls who were coming out and, of course, my mother knew masses of people.

I spent the year before at a convent in Brussels which was a sort of finishing school, and we had lectures on art and history and we'd go to art galleries. Then I came back and lived with my grandmother, who had a lovely house in Chester Street. I would go to lunch parties with my mother and then there was the occasional tea party, which I didn't really enjoy unless there were some of my particular friends there and you could sit in a corner and chat.

The first big dance I went to was Queen Charlotte's Ball. I wore a thing in white tulle like everyone else, which looks quite horrible now. I went in Lady Hamond-Graeme's party—she was one of the organizers—and with my parents of course. It was a good way to begin because you were with a good many people you knew and everyone watched to see you were having a good time.

I was presented at one of the afternoon parties, and wore a terrible dress and the

Left: The Hon. Sallyann Vivian, 'deb of the year' in
1949, photographed with her mother, Lady Vivian, on
her way to be presented at court. Below: Queuing for
a slice of the cake at Queen Charlotte's Ball in 1946.

most frightful hat with barbed wire netting at the front and long gloves. All I can
remember is standing in a long gallery and the Queen just walking through.
I wasn't actually presented, although my aunt was in waiting. We just curtsied as
the Queen went past. It was very informal but even so it was interesting, because
I had never been inside Buckingham Palace and, as I had been away from London,
I had never seen the Queen close-to before.

I didn't particularly enjoy the cocktail parties as I think it is terribly difficult
just standing and talking to people. But in fact I didn't have a dance myself.
I had a cocktail party in my grandmother's house. We had a great number of
people and it seemed to go very well.

But the balls were fun. I think why it was nicer in my day was because the men
were older. There hadn't been many parties and things were just starting to get
going again. I think it must be difficult now for girls who are 18, dancing with
20-year-olds and even some of their own age. Most of the men were army, stationed
either in London or Windsor, or something in the City.

The dinner parties before the dances were always properly organized and if you
were invited at 8 you arrived at 8, and did not roll up at 8.30 as one would today.

73

One was always told to talk to the person on one side during the first course and the one on your other side during the next, and you did not talk across the table. When you got to the dance, all the men in your dinner party were meant to dance with each girl who had been there, and the hostess, but after that it didn't matter. The mothers did not watch you and no one minded if you spent a lot of the evening dancing with one particular partner. But I wasn't allowed to go to nightclubs until later on in the season and then only in a party. Oh, and you could not wear mascara. I remember going to have my picture taken by Anthony Beauchamp and he wanted me to put mascara on for it, and my mother, who came with me to the sitting, was absolutely horrified. We just had lipstick and powder and I should think looked pretty awful.

At the dinner parties you always had four courses, with soup, then fish and chicken which were both off the ration. And there were always things to eat at the dance—salmon and strawberries. And for breakfast, eggs and kedgeree. You only had programmes at the balls in Scotland. I went to two of those but I didn't really enjoy those because I am not mad about reels.

You got to bed about 3.30, so in London I always got up late, about 11, and then there were luncheon parties and you would go to the hairdresser. Otherwise one would shop and look at clothes and really lead a perfectly normal existence. I suppose I had about half a dozen dance dresses and cocktail dresses, and you changed for the theatre in those days.

Then there were the house-parties. You would go down for the dance on Friday and then there would be tennis or perhaps swimming, if there was a pool, on the Saturday. You were always organized. You never had people just left with nothing to do, kicking their heels.

I think the season was necessary in my day, not as a marriage market, but because that was how you met people. One had led an awfully sheltered life at school, which sounds antiquated today, and then you came to London and could go to parties under some supervision. Now there is no point, because people make their own friends and there is nothing one cannot do, whereas in my day, things were plotted and planned by your parents. But I don't think I got anything except fun out of the season. Possibly it tidied one up; one bothered about one's hair and made sure one's gloves were clean.

Afterwards I worked at Fortnum's, which I loved because it was rather like playing shop as a child, and I went on going to parties. But then I got overtired and a bit ill—nothing serious, something like anaemia—and it was decided I should just work in the afternoon, so I went to help at Lady Eden's school. I know I organized sports but I think what that meant was I took the children for walks. But I never thought in terms of a career, simply in terms of jobs.'

Sallyann Vivian did not marry for some time afterwards, and her first husband, a theatrical agent, was in no way connected with the season. She did, however meet her second husband at a dinner party given by a friend she made the year she came out. He is a director of a merchant bank, older than she is. It is a second marriage for them both and he was already married when she was a debutante. They live in a terrace house in Chelsea and have one son.

For the young man-about-town, the season was a very pleasant and comparatively cheap way of having a good time. One such had done his National Service in the King's Own Scottish Borderers and then in 1949 gone to Cambridge:

'Through a variety of friends, largely through my parents, I became part of the season. When it was known I was back in the country, I started to get invitations, often quite blind ones from people I didn't know. There would be a letter saying "I believe you know X, Y, Z. As you're in London, would you like to come to a dance we're giving for my daughter."

It was rather a period of austerity, with rationing, but people were just getting out of their cocoons. They had been very isolated because of the war and I think for the girls it must have been very traumatic to be introduced suddenly to such large parties. In London, they would be at hotels like Claridge's, the Dorchester, the Savoy and the Hyde Park. In most cases there would be a dinner-party first, and as there wasn't much meat you always tended to get poultry. But at that time I hadn't known any different and though I could tell good wine from very bad wine, I couldn't do more than that. But you were always reasonably well fed and given champagne to drink.

The girls weren't very sophisticated but you couldn't expect them to be at 17 or 18. But they didn't seem very attractive to me because they were so young and giggly, although I don't suppose I was a ball of fire either. I was very naive and shy but a lot of them were a real pain to talk to.

Expense never really came into it because most of the entertainment was free and if you hadn't been doing that you would have had to pay to do something else. Occasionally one would go to a nightclub but you could choose whether to or not. Basically it was excellent free entertainment and it gave me a great deal of self-confidence. It is an enormously daunting experience to go to a dinner or a vast party where you don't know a bloody soul, but you got used to it.

It no longer seemed to have much to do with being a marriage market; I think that would be an over-simplification. But it did make the girls more sure of themselves after being cooped up at school, so that later they could pick out the sheep from the goats in potential matches. And it was not at all promiscuous. Of course there was always some girl who was meant to be sleeping around but I think hardly anyone actually did. Certainly I never came across it.'

In 1951, George VI made provision for a return to individual presentations, although only the debutantes actually made their curtsey, not the lady presenting them, as had been the custom before the war. This remained the practice until 1958.

7

THE DEB'S DELIGHT

For the young man-about-town, the 1950s were the boom years. Dances multiplied in number and splendour. In the February election of 1950 Labour's majority had been reduced to six, and 19 months later Churchill was again Prime Minister with a Tory majority. There was the Festival of Britain and when Princess Elizabeth became Queen in February 1952, the press spoke euphorically of a new Elizabethan Age. The country's economic position was improving and by 1954 food-rationing was over.

But prices remained low. Searcy's in 1950 could still provide supper at a dance at 8s 6d a head with champagne at 21s a bottle. Staff were still cheap: the special announcer cost £2 2s, as did the cocktail-mixer. Cigarettes had gone up rather more; they were now 25s a hundred. In the same year, a dance for 130 people, with supper and champagne, cost £212 2s 6d, and this included a full dinner for eight beforehand, with two waiters to serve at table at 10s 6d each. Six years later, costs had not gone up very much. The *New Statesman* threw a cocktail party at Londonderry House for 450 guests and the bill was £604 7s 7d. Among other things, the guests consumed 25 bottles of gin, 12 bottles of whisky and 168 bottles of non-vintage Moët et Chandon at 26s 6d a bottle. Cigarettes were provided. In the same year, a dance for 600 guests at Londonderry House, admittedly with cider cup, although some hard liquor was provided for the older generation, cost about £1,800. There was a 15-piece band.

It was a time when the young men, generally Guards officers or something in the City, could dine out free every night. The catchment area was becoming wider and the numbers of debutantes presented each year were rarely less than 1,000, although not all went on to do a full season. In 1951, 877 were presented, in 1953, 1,198, and after 1955 there were always more than 1,300—the peak year being 1958 when 1,441 made their curtsey in a rush to get in before presentations were finally abolished. The debutante had to be presented by a married lady who had herself been presented, but now a divorced lady, provided she could prove she were the innocent party, could make the presentation. Princess Margaret may have renounced Peter Townsend in 1955 because he was divorced, but attitudes were changing. Kingsley Amis had published *Lucky Jim* in 1954, and John Osborne's *Look Back in Anger* was produced in 1956.

It was a time, Richard Berens, a former editor of the Hickey column in the *Daily Express*, considers, when the season was becoming overwhelmingly middle-class. It was easy to find someone to present your daughter if you could not present her yourself. If you had no friend who could do it, there was always some lady who would undertake the task—at a fee, generally from about £1,000. 'Thirteen years of

Tory rule,' says Berens, 'ensured the survival of the season. But already it was degraded. The very rich and the very smart were already doing their own thing. I used to go about as a bank clerk before I became a journalist. It was a freeload for a whole lot of people. In the 1950s it was really rent-a-crowd, dancing to Tommy Kinsman.'

Television director Mark Chinnery, then a Guards officer, says with nostalgia:

'I probably had more money in my pocket then than at any other time. I still had an allowance from my father. I was in the Welsh Guards with an office in Birdcage Walk, where we got a delicious free lunch, and then in the evening there were all those lovely parties which cost nothing. I was comparatively well-off, although the whole of the deb world was full of people like Robin Douglas-Home who did not actually have much money, although every one assumed they did because of their name and connections.

One was frightfully rude. One would go to all those delightful parties and be so *blasé*. We were a lot of callow youths and we would sniff around rudely, saying in baying voices, "Are you staying or shall we go on?" Then you'd go to the next ball and you would hear the baying voices again, "Monica, are you going on?" and you would go to somewhere like the 400 Club which was frightfully cheap and only cost about ten bob to get in. You would keep your bottle of gin there and just order tonic in an ice bucket. Imagine, gin and tonic at two in the morning!—but it seemed the height of sophistication. I remember one evening when we were going on in our usual frightful way, one older member found us so insufferable that he gave one of us a tremendous kick and sent him sprawling which did shut us up for a bit. I went back one morning to the 400 to collect a cigarette case and it was an amazingly filthy place, covered in dust which you never saw because of the dark red lights.

You got asked to the parties because you knew people who had sisters or relations involved, and at that point you probably behaved yourself. Then it escalated and the poor mothers got you on their list, unless you behaved so badly you were crossed off for a bit. But the best dances were the ones where the mothers were super, because you got rather bored with the debs. Some of them were tremendous and rather naughty and made a dead set for the young men, though I was never quite in that league myself. The debs were so young and fresh from that grim Monkey Club place.

But it wasn't very sexy in my day. Probably there was always a certain proportion of nymphomaniacs among the debs and the mothers. The only pregnancy

I remember had happened to a rather sweet, very grand girl, Lady someone-or-other, and that had happened before the season had even started. But she very bravely went all through the season and it was considered rather chic to know her and she was always being taken to the 400. Later she was whisked off to somewhere in Norfolk to have it. I don't think she married for about two years after that.

It was all a bit rowdy with people behaving as they imagined people did in *Vile Bodies*. I remember one night when we were meant to be on guard at St James's Palace. We would have dinner there and then you would have to inspect the guard. One of us was absolutely soaked and we tried to dissuade him from going but he insisted on marching off, and he always looked very straight and upright. When he got to Marlborough House, where Queen Mary lived, he halted the troop and started to throw gravel at the window and shouted out she was an old Hun. A Lord-in-Waiting came down in a frogged dressing gown and tried to arrest him. Later Queen Mary was very good and interceded for him with the colonel and he was only confined to Purbright for a month, although that was an awful punishment during the season.

What was great fun was going off to the country every weekend. It is only recently I have been able to see any attraction in staying in London at weekends. We stayed in lovely houses and people had marvellous nicknames like Fruity Metcalfe and Baba; and there was a Momo, and the Duke of Marlborough was actually christened Sonny.

The houses were pretty comfortable and the ducal ones still had plenty of staff. Even the Metcalfes, who weren't enormously rich, had a butler who would sub as a valet for the guests. And there were some ravishingly pretty marquees for parties which no one could afford now. That was the awful thing. All those wretched parents pouring money out for their daughters while we all behaved so badly.

Then there was Queen Charlotte's Ball which you went to the first year because you were asked and the next because it was such a hoot with girls taking their knickers off and waving them round and people throwing bread.

The girls were just starting to have jobs, like Caroline Thynne, the daughter of the Marquess of Bath, who had some idiotic job at Rootes in Piccadilly and we would all go past waving and screaming. But the jobs never lasted very long because the employers got tired of the weekending and the hangovers.

It was supposed to be a great cachet if either Princess Margaret or Princess Alexandra came. Princess Margaret was a frightfully good mimic and very pretty, before she got so plump, with those marvellous violet eyes and an amazing drawly little voice. But she was very sharp if you didn't observe protocol.

But though it was fun, gradually one stopped going because you were busy doing other things and then you would get left off the list. I know when I left the army and went to art school I got temporarily very left-wing and despised it all.'

Some of the young men, however, were debs' delights not because of their bad behaviour but because the hostesses knew it would always be impeccable. One such dutiful young man, the cousin of a lord, now works for a charity in London:

'I wasn't in the Guards or at Christ Church, so I wasn't automatically on a list which could be looked up. I got invited by people who knew me or my family. I wasn't the sort of person who would get invited to a party and have no idea who was giving it. But around 1950, when I was at Oxford, I found myself going to parties at Quaglino's and the Hyde Park. People were short of men and if a lady were giving a dinner party before a dance, she would often be asked to supply a couple of extra men. I remember the first dance I went to was given by Lady Lloyd for her daughter Chelsey at the Hyde Park. I had a tail-coat, but we didn't wear gloves, and I know I was round the next morning at 11 with flowers for my dinner-party hostess and then I got invited to her dance. But it wasn't like the old days when my mother was young and she could remember her cousin shuffling the pieces of cardboard on his groaning mantelpiece like a pack of cards, and you had to be positively repellent not to be invited to parties if you wore trousers.

But still, you were not really invited for yourself. I was very young-looking, and for me I think the worst thing was knowing how to get rid of a partner. I was brought up to think it was up to a guest to say when they wanted to go so I felt it was up to the girl to make it clear. It was far better in Scotland where there were still programmes, because unless you had a steady girl-friend the grass was always greener over your partner's shoulder. I was brought up to think I must dance with the people in my dinner party. I was so well brought-up I was always dancing with the ones who were wall-flowers, enormously tall or with halitosis, or the ones who hadn't come out, and then I never had the gumption to drop the poor thing. But I did love dancing and I could never see the point of going on to nightclubs. I suppose my real problem was that when I was 25 I looked 15, and all the girls wanted to know older men, and when I looked 25, I was 35 and too old. Now I have gone and married a girl 17 years younger than myself.

I was always staggered by the people who went on being invited no matter how badly they behaved, champagne-squirting or whatever, and those who ate dinner and then disappeared immediately or got drunk. There seemed to be some voodoo practised on the poor hostesses, and when you thought someone would never appear again, there he would be. I think perhaps the daughters would insist on them being invited and say it wouldn't be a party without them. But admittedly, behaving badly generally just meant going off to the 400 or the Blue Angel; all the set really which was at Dominic Elwes's memorial service.

The season was marvellous for me when I was first in London and had very little money because it meant I always had a free dinner. I lived in lodgings and I could usually walk to wherever the dinner was. I was selling books in Harrods for £6 5s a week which meant I took home £5 11s 6d and paid £3 to my landlord, so I had about £2 10s to spend on myself. But there were all these marvellous dances

Far left: Charles Macarthur Hardy was the deb's delight par exellence *in the early 1950s. Left: Sir Denys Lowson, his daughter Melanie, Mr Nicholas Branch and the glamorous Lady Lowson at Queen Charlotte's in 1958. Below: Mr Nigel Dempster at a dance in 1959, in the days when he worked in the City. Behind him is Mr Alex Mackintosh and on the right is Miss Georgiana Mount.*

and you could take a girl to Hatchett's for 27s 6d each.

I suppose I started going away for weekends a bit later. The worry about weekends was always the clothes, because you had to have a tail-coat for the dance on Friday, a dinner-jacket for Saturday, and a tweed suit for Sunday. Once when I was staying with my cousin, he said, "The butler tells me you've forgotten your cuff links", but I was able to produce them from my pocket. But it does show what attention the servants paid to detail, or snooping if you like.

My first hunt ball was at Shrewsbury and it was a club ball, and the members had to wear silk breeches and were fined £1 for every incorrect article of clothing. At another dance I remember in Hampshire which went on very late, all the servants started to gather like Octobrists because they had to clear up and still get up to do the milking in the morning. But the servants were very conscious of class. You would take various ties down with you and the tie the butler would invariably lay out would be your Old Etonian tie. You had to leave the butler ten bob, of course, and if there were housemaids, half a crown on your dressing table.

I never went to Ascot but I did go to the Eton/Harrow match because my mother got up a party with her sister, who had a son at Harrow. Lord's then never meant anything except the Eton/Harrow match. During the war my mother was a Dame at Eton; that's when I first remember Betty Kenward, who was a boy's maid there. I think people enjoy her because they get hooked on lists. I could tell you the names and initials of the 400 boys above me at Eton, whereas if I said Giggleswick, no one would be interested; I think the same is true of Jennifer.

I went to Queen Charlotte's Ball, which was organized in those days by Lady Hamond-Graeme, who was always known as Lady Ham'n'Eggs and had a teeny weeny husband. I danced there with one beautiful ice-cold lady who was amazingly nice looking but very difficult to talk to. I was told that apparently she was very grateful to me; no one else would deign to dance with her because her parents were paying to have her brought out.

I suppose my best years were the end of the fifties when I had a car and I was taking out the daughters of three earls. But it was all fairly innocent. There were girls who were meant to be easy to lay, or course, but the occasions for sleeping with a girl were very complicated and rather messy. Admittedly one heard tremendous rumours about women who are now pillars of society. But generally it was rather more a whole lot of uncomfortable groping.

Now the whole season seems out of date, but I think at the stage I was around it was a perfectly valid way of meeting people of your own sort. Cabinet ministers, senior servants and city fathers would all be struggling into their tail-coats to see that their daughters were launched properly.'

Probably the essential quality for long-term survival as a deb's delight was non-involvement. Perhaps the complete exponent of the art was the Australian Charles Macarthur Hardy. Rich, with a house near Cambridge, he did at least a decade of seasons. In 1959, *Woman's Mirror* featured him under the headline 'How He Kisses a Girl if He's Not in Love', with the elegant Charles photographed elaborately not kissing in four positions:

'Any day now, Charles Macarthur Hardy, 32, will leave his country home near Cambridge to demonstrate the gentle art of kissing when you're not in love.

For the past eight seasons, scores of lovely girls have glittered in the company of this champion debs' escort of all time. They include Sarah Chester Beatty, Edwina Wills (now Viscountess Savernake) and Suna Portman. Yet handsome Charles has stayed a bachelor.

Many debs have uttered the immortal words: "Kiss Me, Hardy," but none has publicly exclaimed afterwards: "I KNOW he loves me."

Plenty of beauties have murmured: "Charlie is my darling," but Charlie has not yet reached the altar.

How has he eluded matrimony for so long? Because he knows how to remain friendly, but not too serious with lovely women. He has a kiss for every occasion—as long as it isn't too romantic.

When Charles kisses a girl she may hear music, but not the Wedding March.'

The accompanying photographs showed Charles illustrating the 'Heavo', as he stared over the head of his passionate partner; the 'Brush-Off' or quick peck below the ear before the girl can turn round; the 'Cool Clinch' with his lips in her hair and the 'Surprise Farewell Chin-Chin' kissing her chin, or if need be tip of her nose to avoid her lips.

In his ninth season, the report went on, 'He has been invited to a hectic preliminary round of cocktail parties in April. Will Charles the Champ come through unscathed?' He did.

8

THE RELUCTANT DEBUTANTE

*E*ven in the 1950s there were some signs of rebellion among the debutantes and some girls were dragged out, very often those who had a clear idea of what they would prefer instead. One, now a journalist, who made her reluctant debut in 1952, complained:

'What I really wanted to do was to go to university, but my parents did not want to send me. They said it was too expensive and that in any case there was no point because I would get married. They decided I should do the season instead. It was a compromise I resented, and in the end I did not really do it. I went to Queen Charlotte's Ball and curtseyed to that cake, but just when I was getting to know a few people, my parents went off to Chile. They would not let me stay alone in London and so I was sent off to Italy to stay with relations.

I was presented the next year with my sister and by then I was really resentful about the whole thing. I wore a dove-grey chiffon dress, the sort of thing a grandmother might wear, and I must have looked about a hundred, in a pink hat with a little veil, and long pink elbow-length gloves. I felt the whole thing, like my season, was second-rate, because we didn't even get the Queen, who was away, but the Queen Mother. I grumbled to my mother and said, "Why on earth do you want us to be presented?" and she said, "When you are abroad you can write your name in the diplomatic book," which is something I have never done and never wanted to do. There was a lot of red carpet and the catering was by Lyons and tasted like it.

I was not interested in the pretences of social life. We were fairly well connected but my mother had a kind of snobbery. Her own upbringing had been diplomatic and she was very good looking and she had been on the fringe of the Prince of Wales's world, which certainly didn't match up to the sort of world we were living in, or my mother was living in, married to a businessman.

It was all very formal and well-behaved. When I was doing it the ghastly Berkeley Dress Show had just started, but it was considered rather vulgar to take part. It was not yet the time for extravanganzas. It was the thirties with early fifties austerity. I can't imagine what my parents thought they were doing because they can't really imagine they were going to get me married off, although they would have been delighted if I had.

I must admit I did like some of my clothes. I remember thinking I looked absolutely smashing in black satin. I had one black taffeta dress, rather low cut, and I had my picture done by Lenare, and for some reason it was printed in the *Standard*. One man wrote a rude letter complaining about my *décolletage* and saying I was showing all my bosom. I was deeply grieved.

Page 86: Serried ranks of debutantes descend the staircase at Grosvenor House for the 1950 Queen Charlotte's Ball. But some of them were now beginning to question the value of the season; a few, for instance, wanted to go to university instead.

But most of my friends had nothing to do with the season and whenever the doorbell rang at home and someone came to see me, my father was always saying, "Here's another bounder".'

Nonetheless she married suitably enough, to a young man who is now a merchant banker. They now have three children and live in a Regency house in St John's Wood. She even managed to achieve her ambition of taking a university degree by studying at London University soon after her marriage.

In 1955, the daughter of a colonial officer, a Governor General, was being forced through her season. She too wanted to go to university and was doing Oxford entrance examinations at the time:

'I never really forgave my mother for making me do it and we still have rows if we talk about it. I made no friends at all from that period of my life, whereas I have them from every other part of my life, which shows how inappropriate it was. I did not discuss it much with my mother at the time but I must have annoyed her sometimes, because I do remember at least on one occasion being thrashed with a hairbrush. It was all perfectly frightful, but rather feebly—I suppose because I was quite young—I didn't just take off somewhere by myself.

As my father was in the colonial service, I had been brought up abroad and I suppose my mother thought it would be some kind of entrée for me. But it wasn't and I didn't meet anybody. Continually at dinner one would be sitting next to the child's uncle, which was not going to be much use anyway.

Another grave disadvantage was that we could not really afford it so we could not do lots of the things which might have made it more fun. One was always conscious of what one should be doing. I remember the snippets of conversation between the mothers and the constant conflicts between what was right and what you could actually afford to do. I did not like my clothes. For a start, I was fat and spotty, but also they were chosen by mutual agreement or disagreement between my mother and me and I was already conscious that she had appalling taste in clothes.

I think we did suffer from the fact that society was beginning to break down. The old-fashioned thing of not talking across the table had gone and yet you were often not properly introduced at dances because it was assumed you knew everybody. You would go to the dances in your dinner party but they did not necessarily stay together. I can remember thinking it was a point in someone's favour if he actually danced with his hostess. There was usually a phalanx of people round the bar. If I had been the hostess I would have been furious. There always seemed to be a horrific shortage of young men, but it was partly because they didn't contribute very much. Probably it was because a lot of them were shy, but at that age, as it was, one just felt a failure. I don't remember ever not dancing at all because usually some kindly soul, often one of the older people, would take pity on you. And the suppers were good and I suppose the less one danced the more one ate. But leaving early was difficult because it was conspicuous and I never really had enough for a taxi. I was continually longing to go and wondering how long it would be before it was over.

Queen Charlotte's Ball was pretty grim though it was quite an interesting spectacle. A lot of the girls had that marvellous untouched look that upper-class girls often seem to have, almost vacant (I don't mean that in a catty way), with beautiful skin. The royal family have it. In fact, one thing I did enjoy was being presented, because I thought it was an interesting thing to have done.

People were endlessly hospitable and staying in country houses could be awful fun. I enjoyed that much more. You were in smaller numbers, the hostess took more trouble and in any case, I got on better with older people. I stayed in some marvellous places. Lord and Lady Saye and Sele were particularly kind; as we arrived, she was holding onto his legs as he tried to mend the medieval guttering— they were both about 70.

The young men were pretty frightful, but then so was I. The real trouble was that I was studying to do Oxford entrance and anything bordering on intellectual activity was frowned on. If I did admit what I was doing, people would say "Oh, how frightfully brainy."

Afterwards, I felt a certain achievement in having survived—in still being alive at the end of it. But I think it was a fearful waste of money and a destructive thing which put me off socializing for ages. It undermined what little self-confidence I had, and I think I would have enjoyed Oxford much more if I hadn't done it. I think one of the problems was that friendship is based on shared experiences, unless you fall madly in love, and one only met people at parties and never learned anything about their tastes or interests. I suppose one did learn to deal with social situations, even if it was only how to eat complicated food.

I think the mums enjoyed it more than the girls and for my mother it was an entrée for her as she had been abroad since her marriage. She was able to revive old friendships and meet new people.'

After taking her degree, she spent some time working for her father at his posting as his social secretary. Later she worked on the administrative side of Glyndebourne and, some nineteen years after her painful launching, she married a professional musician. She teaches part-time and they live in Canonbury.

Even the outwardly successful debutante did not necessarily enjoy herself. Jane Sheffield, who married Jocelyn Stevens, once proprietor of the *Queen* and later deputy chairman and managing director of Beaverbrook newspapers, was quoted in the *Daily Express* in 1956, the year after her debut: 'First of all,' she complained, 'let me say I think the whole operation is monstrous, cruel, terrifying—and I wouldn't go through it again for anything. There's just one thing in its favour. It helps you to make friends.' In 1956, the *Express* said, there were to be 107 debutante dances and 45 charity balls. At any of them, the debs would have met the sort of 'deb-fodder'

Below: Miss Frances Sweeney and Miss Camilla Straight congratulate fellow deb Anna Massey (centre) on the first night of 'The Reluctant Debutante' in 1955. Anna Massey's eagerness to give up the season for the theatre helped bear out the argument of William Douglas Home's witty play. Right: Nevertheless, the parade went on; seen here are debs at the 1953 Queen Charlotte's Ball, some of them apparently more reluctant than others.

caricatured by William Douglas Home in his comedy, *The Reluctant Debutante*, produced in 1955 with one of that year's debs, Anna Massey, in the title role. His heroine, Jane, however, merely thought she would be bored, not made miserable, by the season. If David Bulloch's conversational talents were typical, her fears must have been justified. Here he is making conversation with Jane's mother Sheila and another deb's mum, Mabel, whose daughter Clarissa is the more usual silly deb:

Sheila: How do you do, David? I hope you found somewhere nice to park.

Bulloch: Yes, miles away, though. Almost back outside your flat, Lady Crosswaite.
  (Mabel crosses to Bulloch, passes him and takes a glass from Sheila. Looks at records on stool and then places them on the radiogram.)

Mabel: Oh dear, poor you! Perhaps we should have come in a taxi.

Bulloch: I thought of that. But if we had we would have had to take one back again to get the car.

Sheila: Really, how fascinating! Would you like a cocktail?

Bulloch: I'd love one. Thanks.

Sheila: A cherry?

Bulloch: I'd love one.
  (Mabel sits on stool.)

Sheila: Well then, there you are. (Gives him hers.)

Bulloch: Oh, lovely, thanks! (Pause.) Are you going to Wimbledon this year?

Sheila: No, I don't think so.

Mabel: Are you David?

Bulloch: No. (Pause.) I went last year, though.

Mabel: So did I.

Bulloch: I turned right over Chelsea Bridge. It took me straight there on the Brighton Road. Perhaps you went that way?

Mabel: I don't think so. We went by train.

. . . .

(Enter Clarissa.)

Clarissa: Jane's not nearly ready yet. Oh, hullo, David!

Bulloch: Hullo.

Sheila: Well, I think I'll go and finishing dressing. You see you entertain yourselves. Now Mabel, will you see to drinks?

Mabel: But I'll come with you, darling.

Sheila: Oh, don't bother.

Mabel: It's no bother.

(After Mabel and Sheila have gone, there is a pause of some duration, during which Bulloch is shy about Clarissa's adoring gaze.)

Bulloch: You doing Goodwood this year?

Clarissa: Yes, I think so.

Bulloch: Going down from London?

Clarissa: Yes, are you?

Bulloch: No, I'll be with friends in Hampshire. Down near Petersfield. I don't expect you know them.

Clarissa: Don't I?

Bulloch: Shouldn't think so. They're called Swayne.

Clarissa (crossing towards him behind sofa): S-w-a-i-?

Bulloch: No. Y.

Clarissa: I don't think I know anyone called Swayne.

Bulloch (crosses L. below sofa): Oh then you wouldn't know them.

Clarissa: No.

Bulloch: It's quite a good idea to go by Harting.

Clarissa: Is it?

Bulloch: Yes, it saves the main road traffic on the Midhurst Road. You come in from the west, past a big place called . . . I can't remember what it's called.

Clarissa: It doesn't matter, David.

Bulloch: But if you come down from London, you'll be coming from the north.

Clarissa: I suppose I will.

Bulloch: So Harting wouldn't be much use for you.

Clarissa: No I suppose it wouldn't.

(Long pause. Bulloch moves behind chair.)

Bulloch: Still, it might be useful one day if you find yourself in Hampshire during Goodwood week.

Clarissa: Yes, thanks.

Bulloch: Oh, not a bit.

9

THE DEB'S MUM

For the majority of debutantes the season was fun. Mothers worked hard to ensure success and the Berkeley Debutante Dress Show became one of the events in which participation was necessary. As the *Daily Sketch* put it in 1955, 'Scheming mothers know that if their daughters are to make a success of their season, an appearance in the show is a must.' The cost of bringing out a debutante was now between £2,000 and £10,000. Society papers could comment with a straight face, as the *Queen* did in February 1953, 'Half a million coal miners are to get 6s more a week. They are the men on fixed wages and not those cutting coal or being paid for what they earn. That extra money will mean higher prices for all coal, which will in time raise the cost of most things and so effect the "cost of living", bringing perhaps a new demand', and in May the same year could report 'Peeresses attending the Abbey Service [that is, for the Coronation] will already be considering what hairstyle they will wear to support the regulation tiara and the coronet.'

Paul Tanfield, in the *Daily Mail*, might write: 'The mental anguish in being a debutante has to be seen to be understood. This week—with the Season fast approaching—1,000 carefully nurtured young ladies are involved in a battle for survival in which only the fittest come through,' but his column was devoted to the same debutantes. Even the more left-wing of papers wrote about them; the *Daily Worker* reported in June 1955: 'The "Stagline", as it is called, is largely recruited from the younger officers in the more exclusive regiments like the Guards, helped out by young men in the City.' In the *Daily Herald* in April 1957, Nancy Banks Smith, now television critic of the *Guardian*, devoted a whole feature to the phenomenon:

'The Season is here. A thousand debutantes with a million pounds to spend are coming to London. The five-star hotels are nailing down anything portable and stocking up with champagne—dance band leaders are practising calypsos—photographers' shutters are clicking like cash registers—dressmakers are sewing puppy-plump girls into Paris creations.

Never have fathers worked so hard to pay for it—mothers to arrange it—daughters to scoop the title of Deb of the Year.

It's the Season: the coming-out of 1,000 debutante ducklings; the social whirl; the Thing; the annual racket under unwilling Royal patronage.

The cost of turning a duckling into a social swan is so fantastic that nowadays 90 per cent of the debs simply curtsey to the Queen and go home.

The rest—papa willing—have a four-month Season.

Cash is the key. If you don't know how to curtsey, you can learn at about 1s 6d a minute.

If you don't know anyone who is eligible to present you at Court, you can buy
a sponsor—from a duchess downwards—for a couple of thousand.

If you haven't a country house, you can hire a hotel for your coming-out.

You could do it for £5,000. But the cost of "coming-out" spirals every year. . . .
Banker Arped Plesch spent at least £5,000 last year on ONE coming-out party.

And Henrietta Tiarks, daughter and grand-daughter of bankers, who is tipped
as the Deb of 1957, is not expected to be affected by the credit freeze.

Before the season starts, mothers meet at hush-hush luncheons to exchange
lists of eligible young men. Against some goes the ominous sign N.S.T. (Not Safe in
Taxis).

Invitations from perfect strangers are already showering into bachelor flats.

During the season, the debs usually become shadows of their schoolgirl selves.
"They all diet," says ex-deb Belinda Bellville, now a deb dressmaker. . . .

You must keep going—to Lords, Henley, Ascot, the Derby.

You must be seen in the smart magazines and at the right restaurants.

Dizzy with dancing, the unchaperoned debs grow gayer and wilder. Just high
spirits of course.

Tommy Kinsman, a dance-band leader with whom the typical deb pretends to
fall in love, said so when they pelted his band with oranges and lemons last year.
. . . High spirits, said the Gresham Hotel in Dublin, when the cream of society
fought with sticks of rhubarb while the "best people" poured cooling champagne
on them from the balcony.

During the Season debs don't work. "They work hard enough writing their
thank you letters to their hostesses of the night before," says a deb mother.

Oddly, employers are chary of deb labour. Somehow, they have got the impres-
sion that debs' hearts are not in their work.

But after the balls are over and before the Swiss skiing begins, most of them take
up a job.

Susan Gundrey (at her coming-out party, a fountain played £750 worth of
champagne) served in a coffee bar. "Tips," she complained, "are slow."

The Hon. Elizabeth Rhys had "enormous fun" driving cars for a London garage.
For two months.

Anna Massey, daughter of Raymond Massey, who was presented last year,
cancelled her Season as soon as she was offered the lead in *The Reluctant Debutante*.
"It all seemed so pointless compared to interesting work and intelligent people.
The Season's all right for people with nothing to do".'

96

For the mothers, as Mrs Harrison-Broadley remembers, it was very hard work: 'I presented my elder granddaughter in 1955. The whole of life was one social round. You went to lunches with a little notebook to collect addresses, not only of girls but of young men as well. The lack of partners was awfully worrying, it was agony. One was always begging mothers to let their sons come and I remember how wonderful it was when I met a mother who had two available sons. I booked them at once. You had to collect them somehow or other; usually you would get someone one knew in the Brigade of Guards to bring a friend. On one occasion, one young man who was not quite a gent came. Then he called again to see my granddaughter and I had to shoo him off rather sternly. None of us saw him again. He was rather an imposter impersonating someone who was suitable for the London season which he certainly was not.'

The ordeal was of sufficient interest for Petronella Portobella's book, *How to Be a Deb's Mum*, to be a minor success. The author was Lady Flavia Anderson, who had herself just launched her daughter. The book was in letter form, giving advice to a friend whose daughter was to come out the following year. Here she describes the annual autumnal skirmishes which were essential before the campaign in May:

'Just *how* do birds of a feather flock together? Tennis clubs in the suburbs, youth hostels in the cities, canteens in factories, they all have the same purpose of helping young people to make a circle of friends, but they do have the advantage of a fixed address. Debs' Mums are migratory, but I have discovered their first flocking-ground is London in November. Like swallows over the Mediterranean, driven far apart and off their course by the wind, we were all keen to meet each other again after the years of country life and matrimony which had separated us, all nervous that we should never pick up with old acquaintances, and all rather frightened of what we should do and say when we did. I can tell you that it is not done by instinct, but by a particular Mum, or rather Super-Mum. Or should I say Mum-Superior? No, the last ought, I think, to be reserved for the mere half-dozen whose Ducal names thrust greatness upon them, whereas earnest application to the job is the only qualification for becoming a Super-Mum. . . .

I can always listen to a specialist, however queer the particular passion, and as far as debutantes are concerned, Mrs Plowden-Petherick is *the* authority and Minister of Information. You must surely remember her as Sylvia Wyningham in our young day? Tall, well upholstered, and with coils of hair which simply balance a tiara. She invites you to tea. I mean she will probably invite you next year, because I shall suggest to her that you would be grateful for such an invitation, just as Lady Sheringham put it into her mind to take pity upon me. Don't run away with the idea that Sylvia gets a rake-off, as Alice Hardcastle will no doubt hint to you. Alice is incapable of understanding a *grande passion* or the mind of a specialist. Sylvia has "brought out" her own daughters, and has long ago qualified as a Super-Mum. She really loves "people" and "parties", and hands on information as to how more people and more parties can be organised with the selfless interest of an archeologist reading a paper on his latest dig, in the hopes that it will inspire others to institute further excavations. She collects the names of debutantes in just the same way that Lady Dolgelly collected tooth-mugs: you never know when they will be needed.

Of course, there are those who do get a rake-off. Lady Edgware made a habit of bringing out girls when I was young, and was still on the job when she died three years ago. Despite her hennaed hair, she was then nearly eighty, so it must have been pretty awful to finish her working day at 2 am, but no wonder she stayed in harness until she dropped, if, as they say, she got a thousand pounds a time. No one ever remembered the name of the girl she was launching, and the annual Edgware dance used to be known as the "Inner-Circle non-stop".

However, as I say, Mrs Plowden-Petherick is quite another cup of tea, and you should be extremely grateful if out of the goodness of her heart she helps you to locate some of your fellow flocking-birds. . . .

On the day before the Mums' tea-party, when I came to decide what to wear for it, there simply wasn't anything. I had a good gaze in the mirror, and comforted myself that at thirty-eight—oh well, let's be honest, nearly thirty-nine—I really do look youthful, at least compared with some of the mothers I used to meet at Jane's school. Perhaps being a brunette pays better in middle-age than being a faded blonde, and you always flatter me, darling Pris, by saying my one white streak is quite distinguished. Thank heavens I have kept my figure, so it might have all been worse, except for the hat, and that was terrible. I rushed out to that little shop you told me about, and that charming "queer" who does all the designing, and his boy-friend who is the expert fitter, both insisted I must be gay and not dowager-like. "Not with a retroussé nose", the former advised me with fatherly concern. So I chose a tiny but most dashing affair in scarlet velour, which sits very cockily but perilously on my head. It will never remain there in a Scottish wind, but is just what I need to cheer up last year's "blacks", and give me the courage to face the other London Mums. . . .

Courage is needed when I reflect that you and I are now what we cruelly used to christen our chaperons: "Benchwomen"! What a ghastly picture it conjures up! Grey hair puffed out over pads, rigid backbones, lorgnettes, several chins. Of course some of the Mums really do look like that, but, whether or not we are well preserved, the younger generation is just as cruel in its terminology as we were. One and all we are known as "Old Bag".

There were four of us at tea. We arrived as lost swallows, twittering (or do they whistle?), but we left knowing exactly where we had to fly. Mrs Plowden-Petherick has remained true to her type: a Benchwoman rather than an Old Bag.

She sailed out to her kitchen for the tea-pot and toast, because her daily doesn't come after midday, but she retains when doing her chores a gait as rhythmic and unhurried as that of a courtier handing Louis XIV his garters. Lady Sheringham is, amongst the many, one of the few to own much, and yet maintain a delightful, human and intelligent personality. She had on a hat even saucier than mine. Mrs Charmers is rather long in the tooth. Her "Deb" was an afterthought. Her sons are approaching middle-age, and she is a grandmother several times over. She is dreadfully nervous of having to emerge from her Grannie-like seclusion into the turmoil of a London Season.

When we had got comfortably settled on sofas with tea-cups and something to nibble, and had discussed the view of tree-tops in Eaton Square, and congratulated our hostess on what a nice flat she had found for herself, Lady Sheringham was the bold one who cut through the polite oriental procrastination and came to the point.

"Now, Sylvia, *do* tell us who is coming out this year. We all feel so helpless, at least I'm sure I do. Where does one begin?"

"Well, I did think it would be useful to you to have just a few names," Mrs Plowden-Petherick responded in a diffident tone. Was she simulating diffidence, pretending to be uncertain of her ground? Only afterwards did I come to realise how very certain of it she is. The reasons for her small deception will appear later. Just then I was completely taken in by the apparent inefficiency with which she pulled scraps of paper from her hand-bag. "Only just jotted down," she explained, "I don't make a thing of it, you know."

We restrained ourselves from snatching too avidly at the scraplets, for, after all, "doing the Season" is only a kind of game, played for the amusement and education of the young, of which the first and almost the only rule is that good manners must be observed. I now realise that Sylvia is such a keen specialist, and in fact so methodical, that she could have produced out of her head efficiently filed lists of debutantes in alphabetical order for the last seven years, and I suspect she is already compiling next year's list (your affair) in her quiet moments. Why, then, the innocent deception? Why the apparent uncertainty and the almost indecipherable legends upon scraps of paper? Because the foundation of good manners, as the Chinese have so properly established, is that face must be preserved. In this particular case it had to be presumed, first that we already knew everyone worth knowing, and secondly that Sylvia's ruling archeological passion for digging up debutantes was only a minor interest in a busy life devoted to more worthy causes, Welfare Councils, Hospital Committees, and the like, though personally I think that helping friends to do whatever it is they have set out to do is a worthwhile job in itself.

I gratefully accepted a slightly crumpled piece of paper, and then my heart sank, for amongst the dozen faintly pencilled scrawls there was not one name I knew. "Goodness!" I thought, "I am a social flop." I read it through again, a little comforted by the fact that Lady Sheringham and Mrs Charmers seemed equally puzzled to decipher what was written on the backs of the old envelopes they were holding.

"Betty Ingram?" At last I dared to attempt some kind of comment. "Now would that be the mother or the daughter?"

"Oh, that's the girl, of course," explained Sylvia, "Her mother was Elizabeth Mackenzie. You must remember her."

To my astonishment, I did. My confidence rose.

"She married one of the Ingrams," my hostess added. "The one with the carroty moustache."

I began to see how the game should be played: a mixture of Happy Families and bridge. "And this girl called Edwina Darcy? I used to know someone called Margaret." Thus I bid an informatory double.

"That surely can't be Margaret Darcy's daughter," responded Lady Sheringham. "Surely she can't have a daughter that age already?"

"But she has," Mrs Plowden-Petherick told us. Names began to be tossed to and fro, and second cups of tea were handed round. We swapped our scraps of paper,

*Below: The Berkeley Dress Show was one of the
events which mothers were eager for their debutante
daughters to take part in. Among the 1956 models
were (left to right) Miss Patricia Barker, Miss
Madeleine Drage, Miss Marianne Ford and Miss
Caroline Dalgety. Right: A good collection of
invitations was a necessity for the deb-to-be. Far right:
Miss Mary Cobett, Mr Vere Fane, Miss Bridget
Casey, Miss Elizabeth Rhys and Mr Anthony
Pilkington at the Snow Ball in 1955. Below right:
Margaret, Duchess of Argyll, still stunning 24 years
after her own debut, seen with her daughter Frances
Sweeny at Frances's coming-out dance in 1955.*

Lady Twisleton-Wykeham-Fiennes
and
Mrs Douglas Harrison
at Home
Friday, 2nd August
at Coldwaltham House.

R.S.V.P
Coldwaltham House,
Nr Pulborough, Sussex.

Dinner Dance
8.30 for 9 o'clock.

THE BERKELEY DEBUTANTE DRESS SHOW
in aid of the
National Society for the Prevention of Cruelty to Children
at
THE BERKELEY, PICCADILLY, W.1
on
MONDAY, APRIL 29th, 1957
at 4 p.m.

3.45 for 4
Please bring this ticket with you

Tea

Restaurant Table No. 71

and joyfully began to realise that we really did have some kind of contact or acquaintance with most of the girls who will be "coming out" next summer. It was no mean effort, because all told there were about eighty names of Debs. I could detect in the eyes of Mrs Charmers the triumphant gleam of a Mum-Hen who has found her way to the corn-bin, and is off post-haste to fetch her chicken there.

"May we write it all out?" It was a bold suggestion on my part, but my journalistic training simply couldn't bear the backs of envelopes any longer. Reassured that her preliminary dig into the top strata of "Debbery" was properly appreciated by a set of promising students, Sylvia handed out a glowing kindness together with paper and pencils. We scribbled madly for ten minutes, and she even managed to give us some addresses. Most important this, because though you may have been acquainted with Lady Leightonbuzzard when she entertained in Belgrave Square before the war, you can't be expected to know that she emigrated via a flat in Bloomsbury to a fruit-farm in Kent, and now proposes to rent something in a mews in Chelsea just for this summer. Colourful careers are easier to memorise, so you may recall that Helen, one of *the* Beauties of our day, is no longer under Arkwright (her first husband) in the telephone book, having worked her way quite a considerable distance through the alphabet and the divorce courts to Pewsey, Earl of.

Mrs Charmers, in a very grandmotherly black hat, had been scribbling away beside me for dear life, while I cribbed her spelling. She seemed to enjoy her re-entry into school life, and presently drew a line with a bold flourish, as though to mark the completion of her first essay.

Then we got round to the subject of balls: "Of course if you are going to give a dance, it makes it all so much easier," Mrs Plowden-Petherick told us. "At least easier in the long run."

I glanced at Mrs Charmers, and the smiles we gave each other were sufficiently faint to be non-commital but hopeful. When I came to write down the estimates for Uncle Fushie, I had a fit of the gapes, and added the figures three times over before I was satisfied I hadn't slipped in a nought by mistake. But I couldn't get rid of the little horror, try as I would, and Uncle Fushie became unexpectedly businesslike and, despite his predilection for Jane, conducting her first flirtation among the cream, made it clear that skimmed milk was all that could be hoped for, if cream became too expensive. I am still determined to arrange something in the way of a dance, but it cannot be a whole one. It must be shared. The burning question is who to share it with. I think all the Mums must be in secret negotiation and, like a Geneva Conference, much diplomacy is needed to avoid committing oneself at the conference table pending private talks. Mrs Charmers and I had some weeks ago agreed to have such a private talk, a luncheon alone together, so now we confined ourselves to generalities.

Coyly she fidgeted with her lorgnettes, and then declared, by way of casting a stone into the pool of our silence just to see what would happen, "I think I should prefer to give my ball on a Monday."

"Are you suggesting," Lady Sheringham rippled back, "That the Sabbath would give the girls a chance to get over the previous week's hangover?"

"You may find it difficult to pick a Monday." Sylvia began with no unseemly hurry or clatter to collect our dirty tea-cups on to the silver tray. "I really should go and see Jacquetta before you decide about dates. It's so important not to clash."

"Jacquetta?"

"Clash?"

All we three guests were out of our depth, and were made aware that only the hostess was an experienced aqualung diver. "Her real name is Mrs Benson," Sylvia brought us to the surface. "She writes the social news in the *Rattler*."

(Darling Pris, did you know any one ever *read* the *Rattler*? I thought no one ever did more than look at the pictures, and on my widow's pittance I only do that at the hairdresser's. However, it seems that the *Rattler* publishes an official list of dances with dates, and that Mrs Benson is a cousin of Uncle Fushie. So I shall swiftly get in touch.)

"Of course if we *do* decide to share," Mrs Charmers was whispering to me, as she made an outward show of copying down Mrs Benson's address, which Sylvia had given us, "I quite see that we mustn't choose a date to clash with anyone else, at least"—here she gave the conspiratorial laugh of a villain as delivered in an aside from the wings of a mid-Victorian stage—"at least not with anyone else *important!*"

"Not with any Mum-Superior," I ventured frivolously.

"Exactly!" She dropped her eyelids and covered her mouth to repress the giggle for which I am sure she was reprimanded half a century ago as unseemly for a girl in her teens. "They were known as the Queens of Society in my day," she confessed, and as she raised her eyes, I saw a twinkle which had survived all reprimands. In fact she is a pet, and I really begin to hope that our association will develop into the partnership of sharing a dance and "receiving" side by side. She is some distant relation of my "in-laws", and that's why we had come to be in touch.

"Now how about these dinner hostesses?" Lady Sheringham was as determined to extract all possible information from Sylvia as a sensible patient would be to ascertain from the doctor particulars of the full treatment, and she raised her voice to make the conversation once again general.

"Well, you can count on an average of say eight to ten per dinner," Mrs P.-P. was replying, "so you could begin by dividing the total number by ten, though you will probably need a few more in the end. And it *is* rather important to have a good, kind friend who will act as a rubbish bin."

"Oh stop!" I pleaded. "Please stop and begin again. I'm quite lost. I'm not there at all. What is all this about arithmetic and rubbish bins?"

Even Mrs Charmers was a little astonished at my ignorance. If she as a grandmother could make the grade, I felt I ought to be doing better. "You have to arrange for the girls to dine, of course," she put in with something like reproach.

Well, I wouldn't have wanted to see the eighty Debs go hungry, but I hadn't realised the responsibility of seeing they were fed was on me.

"So you invite your friends to give dinner-parties," our hostess carried on patiently. (Apparently it is the provision of partners rather than food that makes this move essential.) "And naturally *some* hostesses, probably just the ones you *want*"—here Sylvia became coyly ill at ease, and I found myself whispering "Queens of Society" under my breath—"get very committed, so you want to write to them early, say January."

I did some quick mental arithmetic. If I decide to share a dance with "X", and we limit ourselves to three hundred guests, we shall between us need at least thirty benevolent friends to give them dinner. "But what are the rubbish bins for?" I insisted. My bewildered mind had conjured up an image of rows of galvanised-iron containers filled with unwanted salmon-and-chicken suppers, and it did seem a waste.

"Only my little joke!" Sylvia admitted with an air of dash: the daring of a professor who throws a Piltdown skull into an excavation just to see the fun. "You see, my dear, *you* will have to arrange which dinner hostess is to have which girls to dine. Of course you can allot them arbitrarily, but most dinner hostesses are grateful for a little bit of say in the matter. It means a lot of letter-writing. And in the end there are always about a dozen girls whom nobody wants very much. Then if you have some good stalwart friend as a standby, you can plant them all on her. And there you are! Your problem's solved."

(My dear Pris, I tremble lest poor Jane should ever be relegated, disconsolate, to a "rubbish bin," but Sylvia's next words relieved my mind.)

"On the other hand, if a girl is known to be giving a dance," she said, "everybody will want to have her to dine." She paused, giving us time to infer the obvious that we should all be wiser in the end to give dances, to hang the expense and put another pea in the soup; and that dinner hostesses would compete to entertain dance-givers as fiercely as lions for early Christians. Why? Because on the basis of cutlet-for-cutlet, if Mrs X entertains Miss Y for Lady Z's dance, then Mrs Y will have to ask Miss X to the Y-family dance, even though Mrs X has avoided bankruptcy by refusing to give any ball, and has merely held a few dinner parties. "And so," went on Mrs Plowden-Petherick a little slyly, "if you do decide to give a dance, don't give it too early in the Season. Your girl will receive invitations to simply everything," she cleared her throat, "*pending* the issue of invitations to her own ball."

"Ah!"

"Oh!"

"Yes, I see." It had taken us time to appreciate the subtlety of her use of the word "pending". I had a sudden and horrid vision of Alice Hardcastle's face, lips drawn back to display her large but well-regulated teeth. She was clipping out the words "cutlet-for-cutlet," as sharply as though she had a pair of scissors in her mouth. I feel rueful when I reflect that the world is what it is, but, alas! attempts to revolutionise it only seem to make it worse.

"We allot the girls to the dinner hostesses, but the dinner hostesses themselves provide the men, don't they?" For a grandmother, Mrs Charmers was very well informed. I suppose it is because she lives in London and has heard more of this kind of chat than I have.

"Yes," Mrs Plowden-Petherick agreed; "hence the importance of having as dinner hostesses just the people on whom you can *rely* to bring the *kind* of men you want."

"But how does one get to know enough young men to ask to dinner?" Lady

Sheringham's brow was wrinkled and anxious. Like me, she has no sons to act as whippers-in.

"In my day," I volunteered, "there was a thing called the Bachelor's Book. Your best girl friend lent it to you, and you copied down all the names and addresses."

"I'm glad to say *that* custom has died out." Our hostess's disapproval was uncompromising, and I felt completely crushed, until I reflected that at least the old Duchess of Paddington's list had cut out the goats, if not the wolves from the lambs. Also I wondered whether to believe Sylvia, because her off-hand generalisation wasn't borne out by a certain story concerning Lady Leightonbuzzard: a story which even went the round of the provinces and reached me in the north. It seems that, when her eldest girl "came out" three years ago, she did acquire such a Bachelor's Book from another Mum. Against about half a dozen of the names was written the cryptic group of initials, N.S.I.T. and, thinking it must be some new-fangled degree or decoration, she added it to the names on the envelopes of her dance invitations. Only afterwards did her friend divulge that the initials stood for "Not Safe in Taxis," since when, and amidst general laughter, the other Mums have been trying unsuccessfully to ascertain who were the Black Sheep, with a view to excluding them from nocturnal transport service.

"But then," Lady Sheringham was persistent, "without the dear old Bachelor's Book, how do you get to know any men?"

"The girls themselves collect a circle of friends at the dinner-parties they go to," Sylvia reassured her. "You only need to know a mere half dozen to ask to your own first dinner party, and that starts the ball rolling."

(Pris darling, I foresee trouble over this problem. Perhaps some girls have methodic and quick-filing minds. If so they are destined to be the Super-Mums of a future generation. But my Jane is as feather-brained over certain things as I am myself. Apparently it is going to be my job to write to young men and ask them to dinner. For it is, I learn, absolutely "out" for a Deb to do the actual writing of the letter herself to a man she has only met at a dinner-party the week before. But as under the present system, and since the abolition of the records of celibacy, only Jane can have any knowledge of the young man's existence, I prophesy that she will tell me to invite a particular creature called Tommy or Dicky or Harry, identifiable by fair hair, possibly by his regiment, or the fact that he owns a spaniel or even a Jaguar, but whose surname and address she has forgotten or been too secretly shy to elucidate.)

Soon after that the tea-party broke up. But I came away firm of purpose, and considerably more confident. I have collected the names of eighty Debs-to-be, with most of whose mothers, fathers or cousins I have some acquaintance. I know I must consult Jacquetta of the *Rattler* before I pick a date for our dance. I must now decide which of my friends are long-suffering enough to give dinner-parties for such a ball, though it is beginning to dawn upon me that Second-Year-Mums will jump at the proposition, the reason for which wicked piece of worldliness I will endeavour to clarify later. Sylvia says April is the month in which to send out my invitations to the girls for a dance at midsummer, but that it is better not to invite the men until a month before the event. Really, I have learnt quite a lot in one

afternoon. Heaven bless Sylvia! Perhaps I shall yet rank as an efficient Deb's Mum.'

By contrast, the role of the debutante's father was a supportive and financing one. Sir Maurice and Lady Bridgeman's four daughters came out between 1952 and 1965. But as Sir Maurice, then chairman of British Petroleum, says, 'I kept very much in the background. I took it for granted. Because one had these daughters one knew they would become debutantes sooner or later. But the work is done at mums' lunches. The season didn't involve me a lot because I was working. They did not hang about the flat. If people came to drinks or to dinner they went out afterwards. We did give a few dinner parties, but they were never large because we had a small flat. We had a few young people to stay at weekends. But it wasn't a chore except that they smoked all one's cigarettes and one was four miles from the nearest village. And some drank a good deal of one's drink. But the young men were not foolish, although often it was difficult to find a common topic of conversation.'

But Sir Maurice admitted he was never much of a party-goer even when he was a young man, whereas Lady Bridgeman enjoyed the parties and dances:

'When Erica came out in 1952 there was a real point in the season. Later, mums' lunches became ridiculous, but at that stage they supplied a lack because everyone was out of touch because of the war. There hadn't been teenage parties and you were very anxious for your children to have friends. But you didn't know where your friends were living and you couldn't remember exactly what ages their children were. Before the season, I think Erica knew two young men. It was as bad as that. So, you said to a friend with a daughter the same age, "Who do you know is coming out?" It was as simple as that. You collected addresses from your friends. Then my mother met someone who was having a mums' lunch, in a large flat behind the Royal Albert Hall. It was the first one I had been to and there was only one person there whom I even knew at all. Then a proper list was handed round. It was headed "Jeunes Hommes". Driving away with the one person I already knew slightly, we were both hysterical in the car because some of the "jeunes hommes" were nearly as old as us. We were laughing so hard I drove slap into the back of a lorry. Mrs de Graz had the famous list. She was very helpful to a lot of people and though she did become rather ridiculous, she did it from the kindness of her heart. So did Lady St John of Bletso, who would arrange somewhere for girls to stay if the parents were stuck in the country.'

Sir Maurice pointed out that Lady St John was paid for her services, whereas Mrs de Graz was not. By the time her two younger daughters came out, Lady

Bridgeman added, it was Jennifer who had taken over. 'If you wanted a list of dances to avoid clashing, you rang her up. She was the clearing house.'

Sir Maurice says that he was always very conscious of the cost, which mounted throughout, though the season was not as bad as providing the wedding receptions. Their eldest daughter Erica shared a dance at the Hyde Park Hotel which cost each host about £700. The second, Tessa, had a small dance for 120 people at Lady Bridgeman's mother's house in South Audley Street, with Tommy Kinsman supplying the music. 'By the time my younger daughter came out,' Sir Maurice commented, 'the cost of everything had gone up and they went in more for discotheques instead of the set-piece ball. They both had small dances in a flat in Belgrave Square which my company kept for entertaining.' Lady Bridgeman enjoyed the dances. Sir Maurice merely said, 'One got through them.'

Of their four daughters, it was Tessa, who came out in 1955, who most enjoyed it. 'Partly because,' says Lady Bridgeman, 'she was the sort of girl who enjoyed parties. But also I think it was because I enjoyed it much more. I had married very young and when my eldest daughter came out, I did not know any of the mothers. Three years later, when Tessa came out, they were my real friends. So the other people who came out with Tessa were very much my friends' children. Also, by then we had had our flat in London for some time and had met up with our old friends again and led much more of a London life. But by the time the younger daughters came out, I was saying, "No more mums' lunches." Now, if I had a daughter of eighteen, I am sure she would hate to be called a debutante.'

They both felt that the pre-war years had really been better. 'There was so much more entertaining before the war,' says Sir Maurice, 'everyone had a London house with a few servants and plenty of room.' Lady Bridgeman thinks that everything was much more natural then:

'It was much more an extension of your own life than the effort it became after the war. I had a sister who was eighteen months older than me and we had always had parties in the house. That was in Grosvenor Street. It was all quite automatic; everything was done at home and one's own cook did the supper. Everybody knew everybody. There was never any question of anybody being asked you didn't know. After the war, it was more a question of collecting people you might have known but didn't because of the war.

The other big change after the war was that the bar became the place you changed partners because the music was continuous. Before the war you got booked up, whether you had programmes or not. After the war, because there was continuous music, the only way to swap partners was to go to the bar. That changed the geography of the bar because it had to be where there was plenty of room for all this skullduggery and yet near enough to the ballroom. Before the war, the girls never went to the bar and I remember we were all terribly shocked when one American girl did. We had to hang around the entrance to the ballroom.'

'Conscientious mothers,' complained Sir Maurice, 'kept on introducing one to the most hideous shy girl there, which was why we didn't stay round the door but went to the bar.'

'I think this continuous music,' says Lady Bridgeman, 'was to a great extent why girls got steadies and danced with the same young man all evening. We mothers all used to think, "What is the point of going to all the trouble and expense of dinner parties and dances if a girl was going to dance with the same young man all evening?"

All four of their daughters are married, but none of them married anyone they met through the season. 'That was not so much the point,' in Lady Bridgeman's view, 'it was more that you wanted them to have a wide choice of friends.'

'A lot of the war-time marriages,' commented Sir Maurice, 'came unstuck because there was not so much choice. They just married people they met when they were working, either in the army or in factories.' That was why they were both anxious that their daughters would meet a large number of people. 'It was to meet a wider world—and on the whole the sort of people your parents wanted to you meet.'

They only went to dances given by close friends or those who had given dinner parties. 'Then we'd have a little supper and be home by about midnight.' 'You always wanted to stay longer than me,' said Sir Maurice, 'you always liked dances.' Lady Bridgeman agreed: 'I always liked seeing my friends and my friends' children and my children's friends. Also I enjoyed tremendously seeing the names one had seen on lists and recognizing them from their parents.'

Lady Bridgeman did not take any of her daughters to Ascot, although one daughter went in another party. The girls went to Queen Charlotte's Ball but the Bridgemans never had to get up a party for that and did not go, although Lady Bridgeman had been a Maid of Honour the year she came out. 'It was a rather exceptional charity ball because it was for debutantes and you had to wear white and it was very well organized. After the war, especially when presentations stopped, it became rather a joke because people would come up from the country and go to Queen Charlotte's and think they'd come out. Not that presentations really played a very important part in the season after the war. It was widening your acquaintanceship and seeing a lot of people.'

'One was aware,' concludes Sir Maurice, 'that it was expensive. But I think it was worth it.'

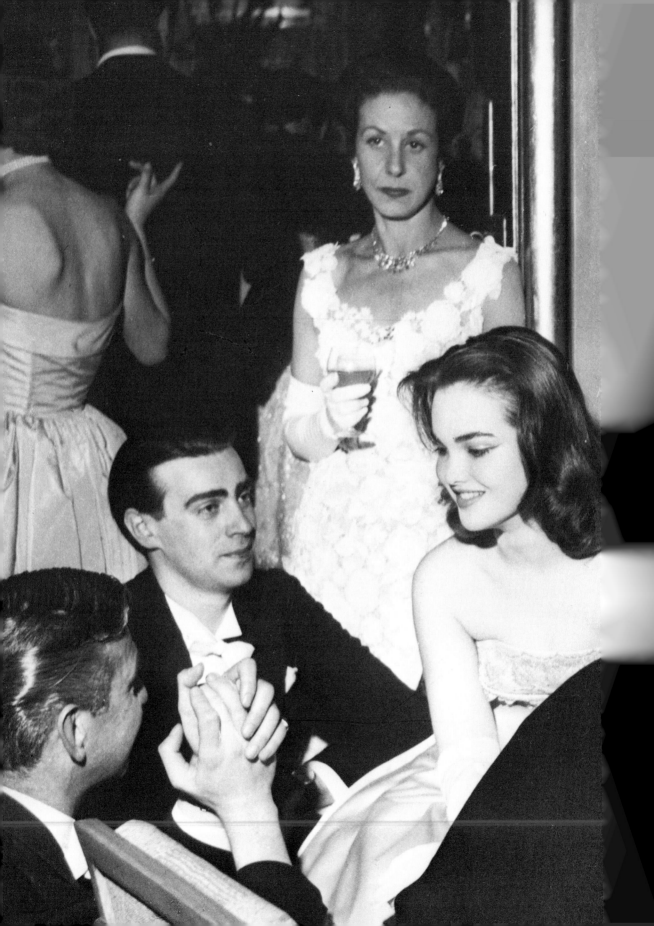

10
'DEB OF THE YEAR'

The year 1957 was a vintage one for debutantes. It was the year Henrietta Tiarks came out, one of the few, and certainly the last, whose fame rests on her successful season alone. She may be the Marchioness of Tavistock but most people remember her solely on the grounds of being the Deb of the Year. 'I suppose it is flattering,' she says, 'that as a result of the notoriety people still remember me by my maiden name after all this time. This afternoon in Harrods, I heard someone say, "Look, there's Henrietta Tiarks".' This was also the last year before the end of presentations was announced, bringing in its wake a rush of 16-year-olds anxious to get their curtsey in before it was too late.

Writing in the *Sketch* that year, Marcia Williamson estimated that the least a successful debutante's parents could get away with spending would be about £1,500, and that was sharing a dance. The actual presentation was no longer such an expense as in the days of evening courts, when the debs, 'resplendent with train, long white gloves, bouquet and feathers, drove up the Mall with chauffeur and footman'. Even allowing for a party afterwards, she thought, £100 could see the deb through that. But a dance in a West End hotel would cost something in the region of £4,000; of which £1,000 went to the hotel for supper and champagne at about £3 a head, with the rest going on flowers, cabaret and orchestra. But most people shared dances anyway, and more were starting to hold them in the country. There were still plenty of people both rich enough and sufficiently interested to spend a great deal more. Macmillan had become Prime Minister in January. It was the start of the 'Never Had It So Good' days.

Lady Tavistock, only daughter of a rich banker, professes not to have enjoyed the season particularly, which must have irritated her less-successful contemporaries:

'The season was terrifying, and I did not really enjoy it very much. Of course it was lovely having lots of pretty clothes, but it did all seem very artificial and rather pointless. I don't think I made many new friends from the season because most of them I knew anyway—I'd known my husband since I was two.

But my mother did give me some very pretty clothes from Paris. We went over and got them from Balmain. It was a year of total frivolity, although I didn't go to parties every night nor did I stay terribly late. In those days it was ludicrous. Until the magic day when you came out you just did not go to parties. It was so extraordinary—suddenly you were "out" and allowed to stay out till two, three, four in the morning. Now girls go to parties from the age of about 15, which I think is much less of a shock to the system.

I didn't really want to do the season but it was never discussed and everyone

111

took it for granted I would. We were then much more unquestioning as teenagers and did what our parents expected us to do. Now with my own children, there's never any question of them simply saying yes, they always ask why.

I think when I did it, the season was a left-over habit. It had had a point and people who could afford it just went on doing it. We were actually presented, it wasn't just garden parties, which made it seem a little better, but it was all rather like being backstage before a school play because there were such a ludicrous number of people. I learnt to curtsey beforehand with Mme Vacani, who had already given me dancing lessons.

My own dance was at Claridge's in May and I shared it with my cousin. I wore a pink strapless embroidered dress from Balmain—I still have it somewhere. It was not just a deb dance because my father said he couldn't see the point of my just meeting people of my own age, so it was my parents' friends as well. We had a band, a group and a nightclub which was very pretty, all done in butterflies by Susan Pulbrook. The Duke of Bedford sat next to my mother at dinner and spilled some champagne all down her dress but she said, "Don't worry, champagne does not stain." He picked up the bottle and saw that it was Dom Perignon and looked amazed. She said, "But we've only got one daughter." Her dress was not stained—but of course no one can afford champagne now.

I remember very clearly how all the publicity started. I was not even in England —I was staying in Madrid and only came back when the season started. Tony Armstrong-Jones had taken some photographs of me and one of them appeared in one of the dailies and it started a competition asking mothers to send in photographs of their daughters. In the beginning it was all great fun. I loved the first photographs which appeared of me in the papers. Then there was the Berkeley Dress Show—I was not particularly flattered to be asked to model for that, I just took it for granted, which sounds terrible—and we all had to walk in Green Park and that was on the news on television that evening which was rather exciting. Then it all snowballed and gradually was quite different. It was horrid, but there seemed no way to stop it. I think it must have been very boring for people to read about, but also it made meeting new people very difficult because obviously they thought, "Ugh," as anyone would. I didn't have a social secretary, although some of the papers said I did. Mummy would pretend to be the daily on the telephone to keep Hickey away. The only time we had any help was when a girl-friend of mine helped my mother with the invitations for our dance.

But the season was frightening. These days if you go to a party, you will usually know lots of people. Then I would know the daughters and the parents but not many of the young men. I was always afraid that no one would dance with me or that I would be stuck with someone quite frightful. I developed a defence mechanism which I used at nearly all the dances I went to; I would dance with some young man whom I did know and like the whole evening. My parents used to point out I never met anybody and I suppose it was very unadventurous of me. My father was so terrified of people drinking and driving that he didn't use his chauffeur during the day at all when I was doing the season. The car was always there every evening to take me home.

It had one lasting effect on me. I don't like to go to the country for a dance if I do not know the people I am staying with. My reaction always is to say no, because I hate being dependent on someone else to take me home. I start thinking, "What am I going to do for the next four hours?" whereas if I know I can leave when I like, I probably enjoy myself. What really put me off country dances was one weekend when everything went wrong. I drove to stay somewhere with three great friends— Tessa Kennedy and Dominic Elwes were two of them—and the weekend went wrong from the beginning. We arrived in a large, highly coloured American car and the first thing we did was to drive over the corner of the lawn as we arrived. You could see from the start that our hosts did not like us but you know how it is when there are four of you who get on very well—somehow you behave worse. The whole weekend was torture.

I did not do anything while I was doing the season. I met girl-friends for lunch and I spent a lot of time at the hairdresser because I have frightfully floppy hair and it was before the days of backcombing. I hardly ever went to cocktail parties.

I did quite enjoy being Deb of the Year because it was beneficial in that I felt I had won, not that there was a competition. I don't actually think the season was very competitive, although there were, of course, social differences within the season and I think one tended to be a little bitchy about people who were being too obvious. People could be a bit cruel.

At the time I did the season, people would have thought it odd if I hadn't. But if I had a daughter, I certainly wouldn't put her through it unless she begged me to do. But I don't know what there is left and I don't know anyone whose daughter has done it recently. Of course there is Queen Charlotte's which was such an extraordinary thing. A few months ago I said to my husband, "I suppose in about ten years they will ask me to be president of Queen Charlotte's Ball," and he said, "That will make you feel old." Three days later I got a letter asking me if I would do it. It was suddenly on me, but I had too many other commitments.'

Anne Griffiths, then Anne Browning, who came out the same year, enjoyed her coming-out unreservedly:

'Before we started the season, I was at Cygnets House, run by Mrs Rennie-O'Mahoney. She had had Princess Ira von Furstenberg as one of her ex-pupils and she believed everyone should get married at 15 as she had. Her great theme was getting married. When I look back it was incredibly dated. The whole idea was to bring us out, but in such a way that we knew absolutely nothing about how to run a house. It was all about how to open bazaars and how to look elegant and how to run social functions. So we had public speaking once a week—we had to take

113

Below: Henrietta Tiarks, reknowned for both her looks and her fortune, was 1957's 'deb of the year'; she is now the Marchioness of Tavistock. Left: Cygnets at Mrs Rennie O'Mahoney's school prepare to become debutante swans. Seated from left are Miss Sarah Rawlinson, Miss Anne Browning, Miss Hilary Laidlaw Thomson, and Miss Moyre Lade; standing are Miss Jennifer Hart-Dyke and Miss Margaret Cooper.

certificates in that—and once a week she gave us a lecture on how to dress. She herself always looked as if she was about to go to a garden party with enormous hats. We were never allowed out without a hat on—and gloves of course. She said you should never wear jewellery before six but after six put the lot on. She was a great stickler for manners. You were not allowed to blow your nose at table; you had to leave the room. On the other hand, we were allowed to put on lipstick discreetly. Then we were taught appreciation of art, and musical appreciation and journalism which was really just a lovely grand name for English. We had the Cygnets Ball at Claridge's, which was killing. That was when we were meant to emerge from being a cygnet into a swan; we came in to *Swan Lake*—can you imagine anything worse? And we had to clap Mrs Rennie-O'Mahoney in. Looking back it must have been too terrible for words, but as we were all only 16 we thought it was exciting.

The season itself was super and I made some of my greatest friends. It started off with all those tea parties and we all arrived with our address books which were the most important thing we always carried around. You had tea and the highlight was always the chocolate cake. Sometimes there were as many as three teas a day and the great thing was to collect as many addresses as you could. Teas started in January and the cocktail parties in the spring. I was lucky because I knew a lot of girls, and also I had been to dancing classes with Susan Hampshire's mother. We all started going when we were about 15 and as there were boys there we knew quite a lot of men. I never had the worry of not knowing anybody and if there was no one to dance with you, you could always go and sit on the stairs with some girl-friends.

There were always the dinner parties before the dances and one was meant to keep in your dinner party, but one never did. One great problem for the hostess was to look after her party, because often all the men would disappear and the girls were left on her hands. I know when Bill and I were first married, we were asked to give a dinner party for someone's dance and it was absolute hell because all the men just disappeared and we were left with four enchanting girls who didn't know anyone and didn't have partners. We spent the time looking for men we could hook halfway through the evening. But it wasn't very successful; they would come back to us after one dance and it was back to square one.

What struck me as being funny about the presentation was that somehow you thought of yourself as being the only person being presented and when you got there, there were crowds and crowds of people, and you realized you were only a small fish in a rather large sea. I wore a grey-blue dress in paper taffeta with shoes the same colour and long gloves, and a small rather flat hat with one of those little veils. We had enormous cars which were specially hired for the occasion. You had to sit for some time on rows and rows of gold chairs until you were called. Mme Vacani taught us to curtsey and it was frightfully complicated because you had to curtsey to the Queen and then you had to side-step to curtsey to the Duke of Edinburgh. Apparently the Queen used to get seasick with all those people bobbing up and down in front of her the whole time so she never looked at you but always slightly over your head. There was this great thing that if the Duke of Edinburgh smiled at you it was because he was so nice that he only smiled at the ugly ones to cheer them up, so you hoped he wouldn't. Then there was this thing about the spoons. People used to pinch them, thinking they were from Buckingham Palace, but they were Jo. Lyons. Lyons was all the thing that year—and Tommy Kinsman, who had a drum we all signed. He had a brother or someone in his band who looked like him and you never quite knew whether people really had Tommy Kinsman or if he was playing somewhere else.

Apart from the hotels, dances were in places like the Anglo-Belgian Club in Belgrave Square. There was a courtyard at the back with a fountain and the men would get drunk and get thrown into the fountain as the evening went on. The great thing was never to be anywhere near the fountain. I think Sally Gluckstein had her dance at the Trocadero, which was lovely. The theme was ghoulies and ghosties. There was a wall which suddenly disappeared into the ground and dinner was laid out behind it. They had had a small chocolate cake made specially for me because they knew I adored it. Everything was blacked out completely and the waiters were dressed in black with skeleton outlines in luminous paint. The wait-resses were dressed as witches and we were all given a witch doll when we left. It was a fabulous dance. My own dance was at Frank Beresford's studio in St John's Wood and everything was decorated like an underwater cave. I can't remember much about it—I think rather like your wedding, it goes by too quickly. Tessa Kennedy had a lovely dance with a nightclub decorated with real camellias. There were often steel bands but we didn't have discotheques in those days.

I think we were very lucky because ours was the last normal year before the great rush to be in at the end of presentations. The only girls who were looked down on a bit were those who were taking it too seriously and thought they had to make important friends. What was fun was making friends with whomever one liked. Henrietta Tiarks was awfully nice but hardly ever there, which used to amuse us because the papers always said "and Henrietta Tiarks" when she had not been at the party. She was a dear person but she didn't come to the tea parties or do much. The papers got hold of her name before she started the season and we read everywhere that she was so beautiful and we were all longing to see her. We felt sure she would be terribly conceited whereas she was rather sweet and rather shy. I think a lot of people are pushed by their mothers.

The loveliest part was the country houses we stayed in. I remember one house in Yorkshire where we stayed with two elderly people, poor things, who, I should think, had never been invaded by a bunch of teenagers before. Everything was terribly antiquated, including the butler and the kitchen equipment. After dinner we were served with savouries, a minute piece of toast with something on it, and then the butler brought in an enormous silver salver and cover for the host and he had a savoury about ten times the size of ours. That weekend was fun because there were three dances to go to and the York races. But there were problems because there were four men and four girls and we all paired off quite well, except that when we got to one dance, it was obvious that one of the men was in love with a girl in another party and he left my poor girl-friend high and dry. We spent the whole evening trying to find another man or in persuading the first man to come back from the rhododendron bush where he'd gone with his girl-friend. One did tend to worry about friends not having partners; every one was very conscious of

Right: An invitation to The Cygnet's Ball. Below:
Mrs Rennie O'Mahoney (in spotted chiffon) between
Mr David Gammon and Mr and Mrs Robert
Pilkington in 1951. Right: The Countess of
Harewood (now Mrs Jeremy Thorpe) introduces
Hardy Amies to Maria Callas at the
1957 Opera Ball. Far right: Miss
Sally Gluckstein and Mr John
Mosely at the Rose Ball a few years
later. Below right: Recognition
from favourite band-leader
Tommy Kinsman meant that a
deb had 'arrived'.

Mrs W. Rennie-O'Mahony
and
The Cygnets
request the pleasure of the company of

at a Dinner & Dance
at Claridge's
on Saturday, 23rd June, 1956

R.S.V.P. The Hon Treasurer.
The Cygnet's House.
91 Queen's Gate S.W.7

Reception 8.15 p.m.

not wanting a girl-friend to get left out. We were very raw and unsophisticated so perhaps we were less hard-boiled. Our girl-friends meant a lot to us.

One problem, of course, was clothes, because it wasn't like today when you can go to a boutique and get clothes reasonably. The clothes were all scaled-down versions of what your parents wore and were very expensive. We had the most frightful clothes, really ugly and uncomfortable, with stiletto heels so everyone worried about their parquet floors. We had those strapless dresses you were always having to hoist up and then the bones would dig into you and you would have to go and take them out and spend the rest of the evening wondering whether the bodice would fall down. And terrible petticoats which stuck out and which you had to wash in sugar water and took five days to dry. Or you had hoops, which were inclined to "go" in the middle of the evening and suddenly yards and yards of whalebone would appear at the bottom of your dress. We wore gloves and the men wore tails. We didn't wear much make-up, very Yardley, pink lipstick and a bit of powder, no eyeliner but mascara. I remember Sally Gluckstein taking gloves for her partners to wear but I didn't go that far.

Things cost much less but one never mentioned money. One was taught never to discuss it and it was a very delicate operation paying for anything. The girls never paid. There was never any question of going Dutch. All you would take was a shilling or two for the cloakroom attendant. We went to nightclubs like the Condor in Wardour Street where they had a steel band, the Blue Angel and the 400. But we didn't go much because the dances didn't end till three or four in the morning when we had breakfast. How we ever got into our evening dresses, golly, what with three teas, drinks parties, dinners and all those breakfasts !

We had far more publicity then because the papers were all very geared up to the season. The *Daily Mail* had Paul Tanfield on the back page which was usually about the coming-out dances of the night before. Then there were magazines like *Tatler*, the *Queen, Sphere* and a small magazine called the *Londoner*. I don't think the *Londoner* ever sent anyone to the parties; they just used to write things up from the photographs they got from people like Barry Swaebe and Desmond O'Neill. We used to play Hare and Hounds on the Circle Line—the "Bayswater Beagles"—and the press wrote all about that, but it stopped because people wrote and complained they couldn't get on the trains.

Sex was very much frowned-on. I can remember that two years after the season a girl-friend of mine was going on holiday with a man and the tremendous shock that caused us all. If there was sex in the bushes, no one knew about it and it certainly wasn't the accepted thing. Sleeping with a man was very much dis-approved of and you assumed you would be a virgin when you married. If you went out to dinner, you didn't think of how to get out of going to bed with him, it was how to get out of the car without kissing him. But one girl who came out with us and was brought up very strictly and had all her phone calls vetted and listened to went rather off the rails. She hadn't been allowed to go anywhere alone and then the next year she wrote a series of articles in the *News of the World* about "How I Became a Prostitute." Then another girl's mother wrote a series called "Fire in My Blood" about how she'd been goodness knows how many people's mistress. But most of us lived at home and at 17 we were very, very young.

I think what I gained most from the season was to get it out of my system. You didn't want to go on socializing and you don't spend the rest of your life (if you marry early) wondering what you have missed. Very few people actually got married as a result, and I think the two I can think of are both divorced. But we were far too young to marry—we were in love half a dozen times during the season.'

Anne Griffiths was doing a secretarial course at Queen's—but only in the mornings—while she was doing the season. Afterwards she worked for various MPs at the House of Commons, including Sir Peter Rawlinson. She still helps prepare Vacher's *Parliamentary Companion*. Her husband works in the printing business; they live in Chiswick and Mrs Griffiths collects dolls' houses. Perhaps her closest link with the season now is the fact that she is still very active on charitable committees and has recently helped organize functions like the Red Hat Ball.

In 1957, debutantes got so much publicity that the *Daily Mirror* invited readers to nominate their own daughters or girl-friends as Deb of the Year, with Charles Macarthur Hardy as one of the judges, and held a rival ball in honour of their debs— with, naturally, Tommy Kinsman and his band. It was still considered a plus if Princess Alexandra came to a dance, though she had come out a couple of years before when Tommy Kinsman had played for the party she shared with the Duke of Kent at Coppins. Tommy Kinsman was still the band-leader the debs most wanted to play at their parties.

'They were all very fond of the latest show-tunes,' says Tommy Kinsman, 'I'd go on holiday in August to America to get the latest tunes because you weren't meant to play them over here until the shows were put on in this country. Oh, most of the girls had a nice time. But for a few, it was a waste of time. Some of them were wallflowers and went and sat in the toilets, and for them it was a waste of money. But I can tell you of one lady—this was another gag—who came to me and said, "Tommy, I'm going to book you but I'll cancel you right away because I can't afford to have a dance." But she put her party in the list and her daughter got all the invitations even though there never was any party.'

For the men, it went on being an excellent way of spending their evenings, as David Ashton-Bostock recalls:

'Just after I left Wellington to go to art school my mother got a splendid letter from someone none of us had seen for years, a sort of cousin, saying she noticed from the family tree that she had two sons and if either of them was unmarried and was available, would he please come to the enclosed dance. There was an invitation to something at Claridge's and so I was despatched. Then the next year I had three cousins coming out, so I never looked back.

The list of men was a slight myth and never very smart. It was mainly used to fob off what one might call the rich manufacturer's wives who would ask their one smart friend to lunch at Claridge's hoping to be introduced to lots of people, and the list seemed to be the easiest way out. One of my aunts who saw it said that the majority of people on the list seemed to be either dead or to have married ten years previously. But of course everyone had their own list of friends.

I was petrified at the first dance, and at dinner I sat next to two particularly grand girls, one of whom had just come back from doing the season in New York. She kept telling me how much gayer New York was than London. But the next dance was much better because it was given by a neighbour of ours in the country whose daughters was coming out, and I found I knew a lot of people. Parents were always bewailing how different things were before the war, but when they went into it, what they seemed to mean was that there were less servants, the parties weren't quite so lavish and not so often in private houses. But for the quality, size, and everything else like the wearing of tiaras, it was far less different from the 1930s than the 1950s would be from the 1970s. One of the most splendid dances was given for Tessa and Marina Kennedy at the Dorchester, where they had the whole ballroom done as a copy of Versailles, with real camellias and box hedges round the dance floor, with arches and trellis-work and recordings of birds twittering, with vistas when you came to an archway. And there was a dance for an Australian girl called Barbara Stanley Smith at the Stoll Theatre which all the papers said had cost £10,000. It was quite unbelievable. They had filled in the whole of the stalls with a dance floor for about 1,000 people and the boxes were full of garlands and flowers and there was black tulle all over the ceiling. It was quite beautiful, although actually it wasn't a very good dance because you couldn't find anybody and the bars were too small. I arrived with a girl who was a very good friend—fortunately, because I don't think we parted company all evening.

Then there was Elizabeth Rhys's party at Apsley House to which Princess Alexandra came, and when we sat down to dinner it was obvious that the waiters had all been doing themselves so well on the Duke of Wellington's drink that none of them could wait and we had to serve outselves. Later, I remember, she ran off with a truck-driver. And the Belvoir dance for Lindy Guinness and Vivien Leigh's dance where there were people like Danny Kaye.

In the summer, there would be something happening most weekends and often it was a frantic rush because the dance on Friday might be just outside London, in Kent or Sussex, then on Saturday night you had to be in Cheshire or Northumberland. One of the nicest things was the chance it gave you to stay in some of the most beautiful houses in England. I remember staying with the Exeters at Burghley, and Lady Exeter was slightly surprised because I joined the queue and paid my half crown to see the rest of the house.

Oddly enough, I think there were very few debs who didn't enjoy the season. There may have been one or two at the beginning but very few didn't blossom. It was really quite good in that way, although it may have been rather cruel, but a really plain, unattractive girl in May was quite animated and attractive by the end of July. But very few married. And it was all very innocent. It would have caused a major sensation if anyone had been known to sleep with someone and if a girl did she would certainly keep it very quiet. Occasionally two or three dances would get out of hand and appear in the papers but often it was just publicity, because you would read about wild orgies in the papers and you would have been there and known nothing had happened.

There were the girls who were being brought out and there was always a slight stigma attached to them—and one did tend to forget what they looked like. One year, one of the bringers-outers really excelled herself. She had three dances for her various girls and all the invitations came in the same envelope with a little note on the back saying, "Dear David, I hope you can come to a few of these."

I suppose it saved postage, but each mother probably got charged the full amount.

There were still masses of parents in the background at the dances in their splendid dresses and tiaras and I think the parents who were prepared to go added to the enjoyment. The mothers weren't all wet blankets and some were very glamorous like Lady Lowson and Margaret Argyll, and people tended to go for them rather than the daughters. Others were very good about rescuing girls from the ladies'. Of course, nowadays the parents don't go so if someone were trying to come out with his daughter, as they used, there would not be much point because they wouldn't meet anybody. In a way the season had got smaller and snobbier or more exclusive and harder to get into unless you knew people at school. When I was going to parties, one problem was gatecrashers because the lists were published and you knew where every party was. The season was terriby easy for a young man to get into, and some parents were hoaxed by the most amazing individuals. There was one young man who claimed to be a Polish count and went everywhere until he disappeared for some time "at Her Majesty's pleasure".

I went to Queen Charlotte's Ball several times and it was very spectacular, but the dance wasn't much fun because the girls disappeared for hours under that splendid Lady Hamond-Graeme. You really did have to rely on the mothers and make sure you were with someone like Lady Lowson. I did not often get to Ascot because I was working but once I was rather caught out, in fact it was the year I went with Melanie and Lady Lowson. I was meant to be in bed with a bad back and we appeared on the newsreel which all the office saw.'

David Ashton-Bostock runs an interior decorating business in Pimlico and lives in a large nineteenth-century house in the same area. He is still fairly frequently pictured in magazines like the *Tatler*. Although he didn't meet his wife while he was doing the rounds, he has, he says, hundreds of friends whom he made from those days—'I keep in touch with endless people'.

11
THE END OF PRESENTATIONS

*I*n 14 November 1957 the following announcement was made:
    'The Lord Chamberlain gives notice that there will be no Presentation Parties after 1958. The Queen proposes to hold additional Garden Parties in order that larger numbers may be invited to Buckingham Palace.

For some time—in fact since 1954—The Queen has had in mind the general pattern of official entertaining at Buckingham Palace, including the problem of Presentation Parties and certain anomalies to which they give rise. Her Majesty has felt reluctant to bring these to an end because of the pleasure they appear to give to a number of young people and the increasing applications for them. These applications have now risen until it has become necessary either to add to the number of these Parties or to seek some other solution.

The Queen has decided that owing to her many engagements it would not be possible to increase the number of Presentation Parties. Her Majesty therefore proposes to hold (after next year), instead of Presentation Parties, additional Garden Parties, which will have the effect of increasing the number of persons invited to Buckingham Palace, both from the United Kingdom and all other parts of the Commonwealth.

In making these decisions The Queen has taken account of the increasing number of visitors from Commonwealth countries overseas who come to the United Kingdom, the large number of people who are presented to The Queen during Royal Tours and in the course of many other engagements, but who are not enrolled as having been officially presented, and the fact that the formal presentation of gentlemen, by means of Levées, has not been resumed since the war.'

This democratic gesture, as it was dubbed, was generally thought to be a result of Prince Philip's influence. *The Times* welcomed the decision in its second leader:

    'The announcement . . . is a sign of the times. The decision is not sudden. . . .

There will be some natural regrets at the change but they will not be widely felt . . . . The present age is one of transition in the sense that the traditional barriers of class have broken down. It has long ceased to be true that the Court is the centre of an aristocracy, the members of which form a clearly recognizable section of the community.

Formal advantages deriving from the presentation no longer exist. The selection of the privileged few has become increasingly difficult and even invidious. The abandonment of a custom that has largely lost its contemporary value is sensible. However, it should not be taken as an encouragement by those who press for a more and more democratic Court. . . . The theory that the QUEEN should, somehow, bring herself down to the level of her ordinary citizens is absurd and illogical. . . . The function of the Crown as a social symbol is to provide someone to look up to and not merely a figurehead made to look as indistinguishable as possible from everyone else.'

The *Manchester Guardian* thought it was too early to rejoice. In its London Letter it commented, 'The girls who had already determined to be very reluctant debutantes may sleep more easily in their school beds after tonight. . . . For with no court presentation, the only remaining point of the "season" has vanished. If, as seems logical, the whole coming-out system also disappeared it is certain that the fathers, who in the end have to pay for at least one lavish dance and a great many dresses, will have few regrets. But for a time at least, logic may not triumph. The applications for presentations have been increasing—and indeed that is one of the reasons given for discontinuing the presentation parties; it implies that many young women enjoy the frivolities the season brings.'

The *Daily Mail* and the *Daily Express* both bemoaned the ending of presentations. William Hickey and Paul Tanfield both devoted their whole columns to the change. Hickey said:

'So she has gone for good! The girl who either through birth, or money, or both, had the privilege of being presented to the Monarch. She has never been quite the same since 1939. But she still existed in a modified, slightly austere way at the evening presentation parties and now these have gone.

In the old days before the war that presentation was the most tremendous thing. There were the official instructions from the Lord Chamberlain—the train "should not exceed two yards in length" and "must not extend more than 18 inches from the heel of the wearer when standing."

For that Daddy raised another mortgage on the home farm. For that Mummy pawned grandmother's jewels. For that, the poor girl who was to be presented was sent to the Continent to be finished, and then pushed, pummelled, corseted, made to have a semblance of elegance and even curtsey, all habits which don't go with the buxom simplicity of the British girls from the best families.

But the sacrifices had to be made for without that presentation, the girl could scarcely be offered on the marriage market as first class.

On the night the girl was to be presented, she would start dressing at four in the afternoon. The car was nearly always a hired Rolls or Daimler. The rush to get to the head of the queue in the Mall was an expert's job. And with the driver there had to be a footman.

126

At six they started lining up outside the Palace. They were well equipped for the wait. There would be champagne, brandy and pâté sandwiches. Sometimes the wait was so long that things got out of hand. One girl had drunk so much champagne that when she went to curtsey to the King and Queen she fell flat on her face. . . . Then came the war. And let it be said for that generation of girls, there were no Palace parties or Prince of Wales feathers. They were in the Services, driving ambulances or working in factories.

And at the end of the war, it was obvious that the debutante system of the pre-war era could not flourish as before. First, there were garden parties at the Palace which counted as presentation, and this is the system the Queen has finally decided on. But in 1951, King George VI, who loved Court ceremony, decided to bring back a modified form of the old evening party. There were no feathers. The whole business was much more relaxed than before the war. . . . Now something of the exclusiveness and glamour will have disappeared for ever.'

Paul Tanfield said he would miss it and concentrated on the cost. 'In theory,' he wrote, 'you girls could only be presented when your family possessed plenty of background and breeding. In practice, it was just a matter of getting a sponsor. Any married woman who had herself been presented could get you through that loop-hole—at a price. Tonight I can almost hear the sighs of your Mummies and Daddies. Mummy thinks she will be able to have a bit of peace and quiet and put her feet up. And Daddy is thinking of those bills. The ones that go something like this:

Ball for 600	£1,600
Presentation dress	£80
Ascot and cocktail dresses	£200
Printed invitations	£80
Taxis all over town and hired cars	£50.'

Certainly the traditionalists, looking back, feel convinced that it was the end of presentations that meant the inevitable end of the season. Miss Betty Vacani, for example, feels 'the end of the courts really ended the season. It continued in a way and they tried to make Queen Charlotte's Ball into something special, but now it is no more than a round of parties.' Or as Mrs Harrison-Broadley put it, 'Once the presentations had stopped, the whole dropped to a lower level. Now it is up to parents to bring their children up to be a little snobby.' The point of the season had become less apparent, with only the haphazard or at least unexplained vetting of debs by the organizers of Queen Charlotte's Ball to control the boundaries of 'society'.

For the men, the end of the courts seemed irrelevant. 'It didn't matter to the men,' said Mark Chinnery, 'I don't think it mattered much to the really grand families, but it was irritating to the *nouveau riches*.' And the next few seasons seemed to justify this attitude. In 1959, the press were still taking a very strong interest in events. In January, Barbara Griggs reported in the *Evening Standard*:

'The debs—whose final disappearance was predicted last summer—are with us once more. But this is a summer season with a question mark. Now that there are no more Presentation parties, what sort of a season can it be? Diminished in prestige and gaiety? Reduced in splendour? And what is a deb? And why?

Nobody of any intelligence actually supposed the whole deb merry-go-round would collapse with the last of the Presentation parties. But we wondered all the

same. After talking to bandleaders, dressmakers, mums, hotels and caterers, I wonder no longer.

The 1959 season, in fact, promises to be one of the gayest, busiest and most reported ever; money and champagne will flow like water; pretty and hopeful girls will jostle each other for the coveted handful of Top Deb titles; fathers will drag themselves cursing and hung-over to their offices after a night of feverish revelry; mums will intrigue over luncheons, and debs will swop notes over coffee. Charles Macarthur Hardy will be greatly in demand.

Strictly speaking a 1959 debutante is now any young girl whose parents give a coming-out dance for her. But no one is fool enough to suppose that will be that. First major hurdle is the Queen Charlotte's Ball. A cloud of uncertainty hangs over this major occasion. The mothers do not yet know whether their daughters have got tickets. Applications should have been made by January 4; most mothers dealt with that one before they sent out their Christmas cards.

The organisers have announced smoothly that all applications will be dealt with in strict rotation, whatever that may mean. But any deb who is not at Queen Charlotte's Ball is going to find her career blighted at the outset.

There are two other balls, invitations to which will certainly establish any young girl is safely OK. One is the dance to be given by the Duchess of Norfolk (a seasoned deb-launcher) for Lady Mary and Lady Sarah Fitzalan-Howard at Arundel. The other is the Ball given at Belvoir by the Duke and Duchess of Rutland for their niece, Lindy Guinness, who is reported to be very pretty indeed. Most mums are hoping desperately that their daughters will be invited to one if not both of these four-star occasions.

Symptomatic of a less-inhibited, freer (and should we say—more democratic?) social whirl, a Chelsea note is beginning to be perceptible. Belinda Bellville, who makes many of the prettiest and most elegant dresses worn by the debutantes, said, "These debs are rather a gay lot this year—black stockings and rather Chelsea-look and much much more fashion conscious—not nearly as worried about waists and full skirts as they used to be."

Rock 'n' Roll is out, along with the skiffle. The 1959 season will sway to the rhythms of the cha-cha. Tommy Kinsman, booked solid for the season already, says so and he should know. He notes, too, that Scottish dancing is making something of a comeback; and he is surprised at the number of people who can actually dance the Charleston. "Debutantes," he added, "have improved their dancing quite a bit."

The dates in those books at the Savoy, Claridge's, the Dorchester and the Hyde Park Hotel are filling up fast. And in Pont Street, Paris and Switzerland, the cream of the debs are learning what to do with a martini and getting their final lick and polish. The stage is set.'

Jocelyn Stevens, by then proprietor of the *Queen*, was fully aware of the power of society coverage as a circulation booster. In May 1959 he devoted an issue to the season, and in the same issue announced the arrival of Mrs Betty Kenward, formerly of the *Tatler*, as their regular social diarist. 'In line,' the magazine commented, 'with our intention of making the *Queen*'s social coverage more comprehensive we are starting in this issue a regular social column by Jennifer, who probably knows more people and certainly goes to more parties than anyone in the country. From now on, as well as the photographic feature of the major social events of the Season, her column will appear in every issue.' Opening his own article on the phenomenon of the season, Jocelyn Stevens adopted that tongue-in-cheek, half-admiring tone that the magazine still uses today: 'The aristocracy is not in the last throes of decay. It is playing more skilfully than ever at the age-old game called compromise, wherein all is saved and nothing is lost, for there are plenty of others prepared to foot the bill.' In 1959, he went on, there would be more than 150 debutante parties. 'The remarkable process,' he concluded, 'not only perpetuates itself but derives fresh vitality from the increasing number of parents who, with money no object, feel that it is essential for their daughters to "come out". And so it appears that the noise the debutante and her parents will hear this London Season as they struggle into and grind out of the many car parks in which they will spend so much of their time, will not be the death rattle of Society. It will be the ticking of the clock embedded in the dashboard of their Rolls-Royce.'

Other newspapers were adopting a similar half-envious, half-mocking approach in their reporting of the parties they religiously covered. This is an *Evening Standard* write-up of one dance in May 1959:

'Scampering deftly along the petal-pink walls of Quaglino's ballroom, a rustle of debutantes danced the chill night away at a party for Miss Kerry-Jane Ogilvy. Miss Ogilvy, late of Paris's blue-stocking belt (she jilted scholarship for the season), is one, at least, among the tittle-tattle of the 1959 debs who does not think that Camus is a brand of cigarettes.

She is articulate. She makes jokes. Her party had elegance (Mr Douglas Fairbanks) and riches (the Maharajah of Jaipur). It also had whimsy (Miss Zia Foxwell). Last year's deb Miss Foxwell clutched a this year's teddy-bear, by name Waldorf, and wore a diamond necklace that twinkled like a planetarium. Waldorf was to have been kept company by another teddy-bear called Porridge, which belonged to a visiting Cambridge undergraduate, Mr Rupert Hamilton. But Mr Hamilton said "Porridge is upstairs, resting."

It would have been so amusing if we hadn't read it all in a book somewhere. Anyhow, both bears were eventually given orange juice and sat at tables to watch the season rampant.

Milk shakes in six colours were whisked into glasses. Silk in umpteen colours foamed about on the aurora borealis of the dance floor.

At midnight, Lady Gillian Pepys entered in a tight white dress that clung to her like survivors to a raft.

At midnight, department-store deb Miss Georgina Scott, a working girl, glided past, her smile still as fresh as a toothpaste commercial. Lord Valentine Thynne sighed for Greece.

At midnight, Mrs Jack Buchanan said she had sold some of her furniture but would not sell her paintings.

And an escort remarked that there were three candles on every table and three candles were only proper for coffins.

Mr Tommy Kinsman swooned us with Life is Just a Bowl of Cherries. It was, believe it or not, a typical deb dance.'

They wrote, a little condemningly, about the rowdier parties. The *Express*, heading their story 'The Night it Rained Champagne', reported:

'A debs' coming-out party at Londonderry House ended with the police arriving as glasses crashed and champagne flowed in the Park Lane gutters below the first-floor balcony. And yesterday, the morning after, a woman official at Londonderry House protested: "Really, can't the bright young things enjoy themselves without there being all this fuss?"

This was how the debs and their escorts enjoyed themselves at the £3,000 party given for 18-year-old Susanne Mockler and Elizabeth Pinney by their mothers. They hurled cushions into Park Lane, then pelted waiters who ran to pick them up with champagne (glasses included) and plates of kidney;

Flung whisky, champagne and gin to "the poor people passing below" and emptied boxes of cigarettes onto a tramp;

Used food and drinks as missiles in a battle royal with the ladies who walk Park Lane at night.

Explained Elizabeth's mother, Mrs Elliott: "It was just a few hooligans who got out of hand."

Said Hugh Beveridge, one of the guests, "I say, hooligans is a bit strong. It was more, you might say, a spontaneous gesture to the poor. The cigarettes for that tramp for instance."

He added that the battle with the street ladies started when they shouted taunts about "the filthy rich".'

Many things still remained unchanged. The Beaverbrook rule, as far as the William Hickey column was concerned, was still no film stars, no pop stars. It was a place for stories about, say, the Duchess of Westminster and not Elvis Presley. Princess Margaret may have caused a minor sensation by her marriage to photographer Tony Armstrong-Jones, but his pedigree was socially impeccable; it was his career and lifestyle which made the match unusual.

12

ON WITH THE BALL

*T*he girls who danced in the early 1960s were not conscious of participating in an outdated ritual. They may not all have enjoyed it, but they took it for granted. They seemed unaware of the gradual revolution which was to make London the 'swinging capital' of the mid-1960s. Mary Quant had opened Bazaar in the Kings Road in 1955, John Stephen's boutiques had transformed Carnaby Street, but the debutantes were still wearing ball gowns. They might have gone on to dance at the Saddle Room in Park Lane, which was London's first discotheque, but very few would have found their way to the Establishment Club (run by some of the team which started *Private Eye*), which was middle-class-trendy rather than 'society'.

The cost of doing the season had gradually mounted, but champagne was still only 25s a bottle. Gin and whisky were more expensive, with gin about 35s 9d and whisky at 37s 6d, but the announcer for the dance was still reasonable at £3 3s, while the poor cocktail mixer was only £2 5s for the evening. And if your father could afford it, there were still plenty of staff available. Searcy's did a ball at Cliveden in 1959, bringing down 68 of their own staff, while 80 more were provided by Cliveden. The bill for the ball, with a proper supper, a buffet and breakfast for 500 guests, was about £2,000. The guests consumed 219 bottles of Moët et Chandon, plus various other drinks including four cases of whisky. When the Duke of Norfolk gave his dance, he provided 150 of his own staff and Searcy's brought down another 73, including a managing waiter and six under-headwaiters, with a butler to announce, rather expensively, at £7 7s.

Showing that debs were still news in 1961, the *Sunday Dispatch* took a look at the cost of launching a daughter. 'Debs are very much alive and kicking,' wrote Harold Dale. 'Father's cheque book . . . is now the master of the situation—the only qualification a debutante needs. . . . About 250 girls will be pushed forward this summer: dances, Ascot, Henley, strawberries and cream at the Eton and Harrow match, May Week at Cambridge and parties. . . . Any parent who hopes to get out for less than £2,000 is deceiving himself. Some will face bills up to £10,000. . . . Everything hinges on the dance.' His estimate, with help from Fortnum's, of the cost of a ball for 400 at Sevenoaks was £2,500. The marquee, with flooring, lined throughout, lighted with chandeliers, would be £300; first-quality champagne at 32s, down to 17s 6d for sparkling wine; buffet supper and breakfast at £4 4s a head, including the provision of silver and flowers, with gilt chairs at £50 the lorry load and the ubiquitous Tommy Kinsman at £100. Even the *New Statesman* ran one column on debs, casting a scornful look at the 'deb's delight': 'The kind of men one meets at these functions are . . . insufferable. They are immature, arrogant, insensitive, callous and unbelievably stupid. Guards officers, trainees at Lloyd's, aspiring stockbrokers, and a few advertising types (very risqué, this) . . . chinless juveniles, one year out of public school, living in Chelsea and Kensington on small allowances from home. . . . Since they are able to scrounge all their dinners from their hostesses, the only money they require is for the laundry and the occasional taxi.' The actual cost of a season, the *New Statesman* decided, could range from £500 (one small dance, no extras) to £12,000 (one large dance, all extras).

Harriet Bridgeman came out in 1960:

'I had a year to fill in before going to Oxford. It was like putting your hand in a bran-tub; you never knew what you were going to pull out. I went to St Mary's, Wantage, and in my year fifty per cent of the girls at the convent came out, although I don't think we took it very seriously. It was the year Charlotte Bingham, who wrote *Coronet Among the Weeds*, came out, and I think that really summed up our attitude. But you went to lovely parties in lovely houses and you did meet a lot of people. I think the whole myth of the season had really gone, but I was one of four daughters and my father had a lot of spinster sisters which I think was a little on my parents' minds. Anyway, we all came out.

I went to Queen Charlotte's Ball, and already from school we all used to go to the Fourth of June. There was a splendid Paul Getty dance where a lot of people took the silver thinking it belonged to Getty, whereas of course it belonged to the caterer. And I remember staying at the Kleinworts', where I had to share a Chinese Chippendale bed with a girl I didn't know and then my zip got stuck just before dinner. We did not have chaperons at all, but morals hadn't changed. If a girl was known to behave permissively, that was a real scandal.

People seemed to think that the season was terribly expensive, but it didn't need to be. I made most of my own clothes, but terribly badly. At my own dance, I wore a dark blue satin dress that someone else had made which only arrived that morning and wasn't a great success. My parents had tried a mixture of places for our dances, I think probably to find out the cheapest. One sister shared a dance at the Hyde Park; mine was at my grandparents' house in Yorkshire, and I don't think it cost more than £400. My father could still get Moët et Chandon for 25s. He carefully chose a night when there were about five other dances so that not too many people would come, but that also meant there were not enough men. There was a large preponderance of girls and not quite enough food provided by a local caterer.

134

Left: Miss Charlotte Bingham, an early rebel, whose book Coronet Among the Weeds *took a caustic look at the season. Far left: Modelling became many a deb's ambition; the Hon. Rose Keppel was learning how to show off clothes in 1962. Below left: One of the most famous parties of the early 1960s, given by Mr J. Paul Getty at his home, Sutton Place in Surrey. Below: Berkeley Dress Show models in 1962, with Miss Suki Marsham-Townsend modelling a wedding dress.*

champagne. It was easy to arrange because we just got two great churns of milk from the farm and people could have milk shakes. All the milk went, and it started quite a trend and other people had milk bars. We had 250 people which was just right for the house. I did have a marvellous dress, a sort of mesh nylon, which sounds awful, beautifully embroidered, strapless of course, with baby pink under it, and tiers of ribbon, very full at the back.

I was always nervous before a dance because I was so shy, and I think at the dinner parties I spoke a lot of nonsense. The young men were always either army or navy—never air force—or something in London, but you never really knew what they did because you never spoke about that. We just seemed to talk about other dances. I was interested in art but you never ever met any young men who were, and anyway Mama used to worry and say if I spoke about art I would never get married.

Queen Charlotte's was the first big London dance and we had to curtsey to that absurd cake. But I much preferred the country dances, especially the ones in Scotland, because your hostess looked after you a bit. You saw lovely houses and I got on well with older people. It was the whole thing, not just another party in a London hotel. The dances seemed to be better organized and in Scotland you even had programmes. In London all your hostess seemed to do was just to ask if you were all right for getting home and you would say yes. If you hadn't found someone to cling to by about midnight, it could be a bit grim. But you could not go home early because your mother would say, "Not a success?" If we had a dinner party, I always tried to parcel out the less attractive girls to make sure they were all right for lifts, but most people didn't bother and you just had to earmark someone fairly early on. Usually most people did find someone to look after them but there were three girls that year, all very attractive, all of whom married fairly young, who spent every night sitting in the loo in their expensive dresses. Although my parents had bought me everything, I often found I didn't really have enough money for taxis. They gave me £5 a week but it did not seem to go very far.

I always went away at weekends, either to my parents' or to friends, because until I was 20, I was not allowed to stay in London by myself. But there were dances nearly every weekend. I must have gone to five or six dances a week in May, June and July. I never went to dances given by people I didn't know or who didn't know my parents. It was mainly the young men who did that. The season had become too big. When my grandmother was presented, you had to curtsey to all the Royal family and they knew who you were. She got confused and missed one out, and as she went out, she heard George V say "Oh, she's forgotten me". But I just went to one of the garden parties and the Queen had no idea who I was. By 1960, there was room for people like the Lady St John girls who never would have been able to do it. That's why it lost its point. The idea had been to enable you to meet as many people as possible within a controlled area. I don't think it really was a marriage market because we were so young but it was a chance to meet people of sufficient variety to keep you happy. I think it was too big and too sudden, but I did end up with an astonishing number of acquaintances. When I look at "Hatch, Match and Dispatch" in *The Times*, I know an amazing number of people—and I did meet some very nice girls, some of whom became my closest friends.

It was all fairly innocent, because at that time, with a certain type of young man, of a certain background and education, all of whom had sisters who were probably your friends, they did not go to bed with a girl who was a virgin. They knew they had to behave honourably. I certainly didn't go to bed with anyone though there was a lot of heavy petting and it was "everything but". In fact the first time I had an affair was with a Canadian I met in Switzerland when I thought I was just in for a session of heavy petting. It was not his idea at all whereas the young men one knew wouldn't have gone the whole hog.

My immediate reaction after the season was that it had been a great waste, and I would have been just as happy to have done something else which cost far less. I would have liked to have done my A-levels and I always regret I never did.

I really wanted to be a nurse but instead I went afterwards to a secretarial course in Queen's Gate. It was the sort of place where you heard the principal saying on the telephone, "This job would mean working on Saturday mornings? Oh no, that would not suit my girls. They go to their country estates on Saturdays." I have never really thought in terms of a job lasting longer than six months. I just floated about, working for a bit and then going off to the country or skiing. I was brought up to think in terms of enjoying myself.'

As it was some fourteen years before she married, a proper career would have been preferable. When she did marry a merchant banker, she still did not quite succeed in satisfying her mother's expectations, although he is successful and they live in some style in a house in Ladbroke Grove.

Nigel Dempster, now editor of the *Daily Mail* diary, remembers the years when he was out every night for pleasure and not business:

'In those days it was marvellous. I lived very well from 1959 to 1967. I was there in my own right till 1963, when I joined the *Express*. Before that I was at Lloyd's and then I was a stockbroker, but you never did a stroke of work and you didn't spend any money. We used to have competitions to see how little one need spend, and I think the winning amount was two shillings a day. The only expense was the white tie and tails because of the laundry bills, but you could always say to the butler, "Here, my good man. Press this tail coat."

The variety was amazing. There were never less than three cocktail parties and two balls a night from May to July. Then there was a choice of country dances on Fridays and Saturdays. Literally one would choose the part of the country you wanted to be in. I would think, "I'm fed up with Hampshire, what about a week-end in Rutland?". It was wonderful. All those goodies and all the things you could pinch like cigarettes and drink, lots of bottles.

In London, Claridge's was always the best if they opened up the three rooms and you could swing on the chandelier. And there was the Anglo-Belgian Club and Hurlingham, especially in 1959, which was such a marvellous summer. The grand houses in Scotland were nice, but always at the end of a very long drive, so you were at the mercy of your host and hostess. The Scottish season was always very grand, with the Perth races and the eightsome reels, whereas in Ireland it was the Dublin Horse Show and a wild Rabelaisian week of total drunkenness.

If we stayed with people we didn't like, we got our own back. I remember one weekend when we had been mildly insulted, we took all the family silver and buried it under a tree—it may still be there. When we left, the butler searched us, saying, "I know you've got it somewhere".

I'd been at Sherborne and then I had a cousin who came out and various male friends would ask me to come along to parties. Then you would have a card engraved at Truslove and Hanson, saying "Nigel Dempster" in the middle with your address and telephone number in the right-hand corner, and your club, if you had one, in the left. In March and April, you would go to tea parties and hand your card out and then sit back and wait and millions of invitations would appear. Unless Mrs Kenward decided you were totally unpleasant. She would send out her list and if you were not on it, it was a bit difficult. Then all you had to do was to get some young lady to fall in love with you and take you wherever she went.

I would not recommend ditching her, but if you did, you had to move up the scale.

There was not much sex in those days. Then I would think only five per cent of the girls slept with anyone, whereas when I came back in 1965, after a year in America, I would think only five per cent did not. It was very hard to have a sexual relationship in those days. And there were very few marriages.

But there were marvellous parties. There was one at Blenheim; another at Heveningham Hall, which must have been the last dance there. And Lady Samuel gave a dance at Claridge's where they only served pink champagne. We were disgusted—"Oh God, only champagne," we thought. We danced to Tommy Kinsman, Ian Stewart and Russ Henderson and his West Indians.

It was still the post-war formalities. It was only in 1960 that you did not have to wear white tie *de rigeur*. People still sent their sons to Eton, because it was the only school and they hadn't heard of places like Millfield. It was still in the boom years when people could sell off a bit of stock at a vast profit and they didn't have to live off capital.'

Sally Raphael (now Mrs Simon Spenser) was one of those who had a very splendid dance:

'I treated doing the season as a matter of course; both my sisters had done it. When I got back from finishing school in Paris, my mother had arranged everything. I seemed to go to anything and everything that went on, starting with the tea parties. My sisters had been presented but I didn't mind missing the courts; I don't think the end of them had any effect.

Once the tea parties had fizzled out, there were the cocktail parties and then the Berkeley Dress Show—I was a model—and Queen Charlotte's. That was a bit of a giggle, but I didn't really enjoy it because I didn't know many people. Then there were the dances and the dinner parties. Those so much depended on who was there, and they could be a bit sticky, especially if the people at the dinner didn't think it was their duty to give you a dance. But girl-friends were a great help, and I never had to sit out alone.

The season got better as it went along. My own party was at the Dorchester on June 7th and my mother had fixed all that. It was very exotic with flowers and butterflies, very lush and green, done by Lady Pulbrook. But I don't think you every really enjoy your own parties because you are rather on edge.

I enjoyed meeting people and I gained from that and made some good friends, mainly girls. I got extremely tired but not bored, except with those endless fittings for clothes. I didn't think it was a waste of money because I had not known many people before, but by the time my daughters are grown up I doubt whether there will be a season at all. It is not that I disapprove of it, but times have altered. Anyway, there is not much chance of being able to afford it once one has managed to pay for their education. If there were any money left, it would be better spent on travel.'

As an advertisement for the season as a marriage market, Mrs Spencer won't really do. She met her husband, then in the navy, when she was on a trip to Australia. On the other hand, they live very comfortably in a large house near the Boltons. Mrs Spencer would like to work once her three children are at school, but in common with other debs she received no proper formal training. Before her marriage, she worked for an interior decorator and then in Presents of Sloane Street.

But in the 1960s, ambitious mothers still thought that the best route upwards for their daughters was the social one. 'These only allowed their daughters to meet the very glossiest of men,' Hugo Morley-Fletcher, now a director of Christie's, remembers, 'one certainly forced her daughter into a desperately unhappy marriage. But the mother had produced such a good product that although the first marriage broke up, the daughter succeeded in marrying someone even grander and richer the second time round.'

That, however, was only one side of it:

'It was actually a marvellous way of meeting people, although sometimes you felt the dances were a waste of time and money. The girls were not as empty-headed and silly as I had expected. Really, the dinner parties were more enjoyable than the dances, and often everyone felt it was a nuisance when you had to leave to go to the dance.

The weekend parties were the last survival of the proper weekend party, though this did mean the bread-and-butter chore. For a weekend it might mean four letters, because you could have stayed in one house, dined in another, gone to a dance in a third and then lunched in a fourth. Best of all was the Scottish part, which was rather old-fashioned with programmes, although it was often rather shattering because you knew you wouldn't be in bed till 5.30 in the morning and as you left to go to the dance, your host would say, "By the way, we're grouse shooting at 8.30."

It was a way of putting young daughters in the way of suitable people, though for some it didn't work. I remember going to the Harlot's Hop with Lady St John of Bletso and there was this pathetic little hirsute girl whose parents had handed her over to Lady St John, and presumably been told never to appear themselves. This poor child was speechless, short and furry, and not a success.'

The mothers still worked hard and often enjoyed it, like top fashion model Barbara Goalen (Mrs Nigel Campbell), whose daughter Sarah was one of the top debs of 1962:

'When she came out everyone was doing it, so we took it for granted. I was young enough to enjoy it. I loved the dinner parties and the dances. It was very gay. It was the year of the Twist. I only went to one mothers' lunch party, but it didn't seem to make the slightest difference. We didn't have a dance, just a large cocktail party at home here in Chester Square, but Sarah was asked to everything. She knew lots of people because she had been at Lady Eden's school, Fritham House, and then to finishing school in Paris. I suppose she had about seventy-five dresses.

That was the year I organized the Berkeley Dress Show, and instead of going to a *couturier* I went to the ready-to-wear manufacturers. The *Sunday Times* said I had organized it in my "autocratic way". It was very hard work because I chose everything—the shoes, the jewellery. But it was worth it.

But now children are much more independent and the season seems terribly old-fashioned. My two younger daughters pour scorn on the whole idea.'

13
NO CHANGE

*T*he winter of 1962/3 was the great freeze, and unemployment rose to 900,000. *That Was The Week That Was* became required viewing. The Beatles were topping the hit parade and the first rumblings of the Profumo scandal were making themselves heard. But the revelations of high-jinks at Cliveden had no affect on the London season.

After attending a finishing school in Paris, the daughter of an army officer came to London to be launched, rather nervously, into a round of tea parties:

'I was very mousy and quite frightened, but they turned out to be rather fun. I like girls, and they were a lot nicer than I had imagined, and I love tea and cake. Everybody made an effort to have delicious things to eat. There was quite a lot of bitching, but not much at that point, because everybody was still rather uncertain of themselves. You could already pick out the girls who were going to be the shining lights whom we looked on with awe. It was a combination of looks or dressing well, or the confidence that gave them. But some of them had style rather than money or beauty. The tea parties started off by being with the girls you knew already—about fourteen out of the twenty girls at my finishing school were doing the season—and meanwhile mothers were going to lunches and you would get invitations out of the blue from someone your mother had met. I was lucky because my mother had a fanatic interest in clothes and was very helpful, because we dressed smartly. We got up smart.

The first big dance was Queen Charlotte's, which was quite miserable. I was brought up in the usual English way so that one didn't know any men, and you went with people who had been invited because they were sons or brothers. You didn't know them and you took a quick look at them and decided you didn't want to know them, and they were probably doing the same thing about you. Before you had built up a nucleus of friends, there were these awful evenings of peering at everybody and rejecting them. The men were very much part of that scene, and once you had left that world, you tended not to keep up friendships with them. They seemed to be a special breed of men—extraordinary, quite entertaining, and they could dance well, but some of them were obviously just there for the food and the drink. I used to think some of them were extremely old, I imagine they must have been all of 40, and you would look at them and wonder what on earth were they doing there. Looking back, I can see they were the sort of men who weren't likely to have a very fulfilled sex-life, which is why they were there. Because sex didn't come into it, though as the year went on it did get sexier. But it would always have been quite difficult because most girls were living at

home, and at weekends you usually shared a bedroom with another girl. There
were people one knew were sleeping around, and of course if there was bitching,
that was the subject people bitched about most.

The season was still very much a coming-out into the world, because I had never
been to a dance before. I somehow thought it was the start of one's life and it
would go on like that. I went to the hairdresser twice a week—I can't believe it
now, but the cost of the season never entered my head. I had about five long
dresses and then a couple of skirts and tops, and there was a lot of changing of
tops and doing your hair differently and wearing of beads to try and make people
believe you were wearing a different dress. I'd get up late and on a good high-
season day there might be lunch at the Ritz with a couple of mothers and then tea
with a couple of girl friends, because somehow you had got into the way of having
tea. Then you would change for a cocktail party, and if you were going on to a
dance you would wear whatever you were going to wear for that. You'd spend
hours getting dressed and altering your hair and your make-up and having long
baths in delicious-smelling things.

When you got to the cocktail party there was always champagne, and you got
rather *blasé* about it and you often had soft drinks instead. Then you'd go on to
the dinner parties where you were always fed superbly, often with things you
didn't appreciate at all. I can remember thinking, "Oh, not smoked salmon again,"
whereas now I'd give my eye-teeth to have it more than once a week. And all this
eyeing of one another would be going on throughout dinner, while the poor father
would be at one end of the table, often desperately tired, yawning his head off
with the effort of talking to all these inane people. The mother was perhaps rather
enjoying it, depending on how sophisticated the young men on either side of her
were. There were a lot of assiduous mother-polishers among the young men.

Then came the dance, and there would be that uncomfortable moment when,
perfectly often, the men would just disappear. Say the dinner party had not been
quite what they hoped, they would just melt away, leaving you talking in a
hysterical fashion to another girl as if that was the only reason you had come to the
dance, meanwhile nervously darting glances to see if there was anyone there that
you knew at all. If it were too desperate, you'd go off to the ladies' to polish up
things which didn't need polishing up, which took a long time, and you would
hope when you came back the situation would have changed. But there were people,
and I have been among them, who spent the whole evening in the loo. I didn't
do it often, thank God, but there were people who did, not because they were any

144

less nice or less pretty, but because the people they knew hadn't materialized or had found someone else that they really fancied. It was very destructive, that, one of the crueller aspects. I spent one complete evening in the loo at the Dorchester. It was rather a large ball and the ladies' was quite a long way from it, down a long corridor, and you felt very foolish if you had to negotiate it more than twice. That time was awful because I had nothing to read and there was not even another girl there. It was horrid, because you always get that sort of smell in the loo and you've got people coming in and out all the time. There was this kind of friendly thing that the girls would stop and chat to you. But you couldn't go home too early because if you were living with your parents, it made them unhappy to think you had had a miserable time. After that I got a larger evening bag and kept something to read in there.

But generally I was enjoying myself wholeheartedly. I did most of the official things like Ascot and the Fourth of June and the Dublin Horse Show. I'm Irish and I had my dance there and Dublin is a good place to be gay in. We had about fourteen people to stay for the dance, and I suppose about 100 people came. By then I knew the people I wanted to have, though scraping up fifty men did mean getting a few people's cousins and someone who knew someone at Oxford. We had a band and a group. We had local caterers and there was a groaning spread of salmon (of course), ham and turkeys. It looked marvellous, in a stripey marquee with flowers twining round the poles.

I think nowadays girls are more sophisticated and would question whether it was the right thing to do, and in any case they would be bored stiff because they would have done so much already. But you were always wondering who you would meet, and you had the feeling that this weekend there would be a delicious man who was going to sweep you off your feet. There were lovely dances at weekends with house-parties given by poor people to all us boorish, unappreciative young things.

I simply loved it. I have marvellous memories and, well, I'm dotty about the Ritz, and to have the Ritz as part of my daily life was quite fantastic. It was completely useless, completely artificial, completely enjoyable. I think I mainly enjoyed it because I am terribly greedy and there was such lovely food, marvellous breakfasts. So often the food was not really appreciated. Right in the middle of the season there were five dances in a row at Hurlingham, and on the first night I stuck a toothpick into the decorated ham. It reappeared every night with my toothpick in it and it never seemed to get any smaller—and probably each of the people had paid for it. It was always in the same place in the buffet as if it hadn't moved at all, though obviously they'd brushed down the tablecloth and relaid the tables.'

She was studying Spanish and went on to do a minor degree. Her husband is a barrister and has nothing whatsoever to do with the world of the season, she says firmly. In fact he rather disapproved of the whole concept and it is now a completely remote memory to her. Their Georgian house in Wandsworth has a relaxed family feel to it and the baby crawls round the kitchen floor, opening the cupboards. She was measuring out ingredients for the Christmas cake while she thought longingly of her teas at the Ritz.

Claudia Stewart-Richardson (now Mrs Anthony Wainwright) came out the same year. She is the daughter of a Scottish baronet and business man, now dead, and her mother is Irish:

'I think my parents were a bit jumpy about me and thought I had been going round with a whole lot of beatniks. I had a smashing time. I never went to tea parties and my mother didn't like London so she never came. We didn't have a flat, I just had a basement hovel which I was sharing and which I never let anyone come to. The other people were frightfully grand, and not only did they have their palace in the country but they would have a rather nice flat in central London. I was working. My school career kept ending rather rapidly and at least if I were doing the season my parents thought they would have some idea of what I was up to. I was assistant public relations officer at the Institute of Chartered Accountants. It was a smashing job, not at all hard, and then I had all those wonderful parties in the evening.

The only organizing my mother did was the dance I shared with two friends near Windsor for about 300 or 400 people. But she wouldn't go to lunch parties, unless it was friends near home, so she didn't really promote me. It didn't cost very much. I know a lot of people must have spent a hell of a lot, but the most expensive thing is the dance, and if you have it in someone's house and share it, it keeps the cost down. I don't think ours cost more than £120 each.

Even though I wasn't really involved in a big way, there were dances every night and I was away each weekend. You got invitations out of the blue. People would look you up, and if they decided you were respectable they would invite you, though I didn't go unless I did know them or they were in some way connected with the family. But 60 per cent of the invitations came out of the blue—just think what it must have cost them!

I didn't have masses of clothes. They were mostly made by Mum. I didn't madly care what I looked like, although there was a lot of competition. Some of the girls were unbelievably beautiful and spent all their time in the hairdresser, whereas all I got was the occasional quick hair-chop from my Mum.

You had the dinners first, rather funny dinner parties and you could determine by your dinner party if the dance was going to be fun or if it would be ghastly. Some friend of the family giving the dance would give a dinner party without your ever having met them, and then you'd be rather stuck with the other people in the dinner party. It was a bit frowned on if you didn't stay in it, because you upset the numbers. The dinners were very grand, with maids trotting round and rows and rows of knives and forks. Always sherry with the soup, and marvellous wines—and we were only 17. My father nearly had a fit because he didn't think anyone should drink anything except beer till they were 21. Then at the dance you got breakfast—one of the nicest bits was bacon and eggs at 3.30 in the morning.

I had a group of friends who were quite crazy and badly behaved, and people wouldn't have them in their houses because they would get drunk and break up the furniture. One staying with us came back late, climbed through the bathroom window, fell in the loo and was so drunk he couldn't get out. I ran round Hyde Park Corner in my nightie for a bet, and one night I jumped into the Thames outside the Savoy. My mother was furious because it was in a dress she'd just made me. People were always telling her they had heard I'd behaved incredibly badly at Lord so-and-so's dance: But we weren't at all a permissive society—that's much more recent.'

Her mother remembers some of Claudia's other exploits with horrified amusement. When they read in the local paper that Claudia was to be Lady Godiva in a local event, they telegrammed 'Don't', and managed to stop her. But they were not taking Claudia's coming-out very seriously; one of the young men her mother thinks of as being the most amusing confided to her that he got on the list by selecting the name of a hostess who had given a dance from *The Times* and sending her a dozen red roses with a polite thank-you letter. After that, he had been invited everywhere.

'I did go to the Fourth of June,' Claudia added, 'because we had a horse and it was near home. Weekends were lovely and so well organized it was incredible. Someone would ring up and say he was driving to so-and-so's dance and did you want a lift. I always felt rather sorry for the people who had to have house parties for those people they didn't know and who weren't particularly nice. Some of the men, my God, they were wet and chinless. People were often rather desperate for men, and no man between 20 and 35 was too miserable not to be grabbed. There were aimless young men in London who were around and eligible.'

Rather scathingly, she cheerfully included her own husband Anthony and his brother as examples of the aimless young-men-about-town. But she didn't meet him through the season, as she already knew him from home. Until recently he worked as an executive for Thomson Regional Newspapers and she helped run the properties of a small company. But last winter they decided to let their house in Fulham and went off to work for the British Ski Club in Switzerland.

'I had a lot of fun but I don't think the season in my day really had any point. It was really a herding of cattle, herding your daughters together to get them off your hands and to try and find them some nice rich men somewhere with estates. But I loved rushing home from work, putting on another home-made dress and rushing off to another dance. I'm pretty gregarious, and the louder the music and the longer it went on the more I liked it. Often I didn't go to bed at all. I would sit around smoking cigarettes and drinking black coffee until it was time to go to work.

There was a nasty snobby side to it because you really did know from the kind of party people gave and the clothes they wore exactly what their father's income was. Some were incredibly rich; one girl had a selection of tiaras and furs. People were always talking about the dances afterwards and often trying to outdo the next person. There was the extravagant dance Paul Getty gave for Jessica Kitson. I don't remember it being a fantastic dance; one just was aware how much money it must have cost with caviar and champagne and a funfair.

Some girls didn't enjoy it. At that age, turning out to a large ball and not knowing people and coming from the country was quite scary if there was no dinner party beforehand, and there were always a couple of tearful girls in the loo. Some people must have loathed it. If you weren't attractive and didn't have nice clothes or your father didn't have a title, you could forget it unless you had the personality to carry it off. People were very much judged by who they were and what they wore, that was the nasty side of it.'

Princess Alexandra Galitzine, who came out in 1964, thinks that already there was a transitional feel about it:

*Below : Some of the 80 hopeful debutantes who went
to the Berkeley Hotel in 1963 to see if they would be
among those chosen to model. Bottom : Princess
Alexandra Galitzine with Mr Michael Wordsworth
at a dance given for Miss Rose Price in 1964. The
ballroom had been transformed into a French café
scene for the occasion. Right : Formal ball gowns were
still* de rigueur *for Queen Charlotte's Ball in 1964.*

'When I did it, it was both upper-class ladies launching their lovely daughters into society and self-made people trying to get in for totally different reasons. I remember one dance in particular at the Dorchester where I didn't know the girl who had invited me and none of my friends knew who she was, and this was quite late in the season when you did know most people. But we decided to accept, and I even got invited to the family dinner beforehand and none of us even knew whom to say hullo to when we arrived. When we did meet the girl—I think she was from some Jewish family who had made a lot of money—she turned out to be very sweet, but that was the only time she was heard of that season and yet she had this enormous dance. There were people who would advise poor girls like that.

I always preferred the London parties because I knew I could get into a taxi and go home after half an hour if I wished. I was rather reluctant to accept country invitations because you were so dependent on your hostess.

My mother had not wanted me to do the season but my father did. He thought it would give me an entrée into London because I had been living in the country and also that it was the right thing to do—there was certainly an element of that. My parents are divorced, so it was my father who was at the heart of the whole thing. He used to adore going to mums' lunches and being the only man there. But my mother just thought it was a great waste of money, though I have no idea what it did cost.

I seldom went to cocktail parties. I went to one tea party in my jeans but I couldn't take all those little ladies in their twin-sets and pearls. My father paid for my dance but I organized it and passed out at it. It was at his flat in London, and because it was in a confined space I think there were only about 120 people. Because my father was at work and my mother in the country, I had to arrange the catering and the drink and everything. I had some friends who were jazz musicians who came and played and there was a discotheque. It was all quite good and I passed out stoned at 2.30 in the morning after three glasses of neat vodka. I did it quite graciously. I excused myself from whoever I was dancing with and went into the bedroom and knew nothing till 4.30 in the afternoon. It was a good way to go.'

Jennifer's account read, 'Later in the evening I went to the dance Prince Yuri Galitzine gave for his very attractive daughter, Miss Alexandra Galitzine, who received the guests with him and her mother, Mrs Bruno de Hamel. When I arrived, the ballroom was packed with happy young friends who danced until the early hours to music supplied by Charles Cary Elwes and his trio, and Mr Robert Morrison and his very good Discotheque Service. There were several rooms for sitting out and a supper room. . . . Among friends I met Mrs Guy Holland, Mrs Penelope Kitson, Mr and Mrs Peter Kenyon and the Hon Michael and Mrs Hopwood, who had all given dinner parties for the dance.'

Alex Galitzine says she does not now regret doing the season,

'But I met an awful lot of people I never want to see again, and I found the constant competition between the girls about how many dresses one had and how many dances one had been invited to very unpleasant. We were rather an un-attractive bunch, as dear Betty Kenward told us time and time again in her column. In retrospect, even a couple of years later, we used to laugh about it; we were unattractive because fashions were going through a tremendous upheaval at the time and it fell to us to wear the most ghastly dresses. It was right in the middle of the change from old-fashioned ball-gowns to people beginning to look much more casual. If anyone did arrive anywhere looking stunning, Betty Kenward would always pounce on it and say how lovely she had looked.

There was usually only one party each night but there was one every night, and physically it was not just possible to go to them all. I went to Queen Charlotte's Ball and left at the Cinderella hour through sheer boredom. God, it was a terrible evening. In London I always slept in late, and there would be lunch parties and I was constantly going to the hairdresser to have my hair brushed out or put up. I continually thought what a waste of money it all was, but being a lazy person by nature it was a marvellous excuse to enjoy oneself and not work.

I went to most of the seasonal functions, but not Ascot, because racing does not interest me. I went to the May Balls in Cambridge and was so physically exhausted I couldn't go to Oxford, and I stayed in bed for three days. I went to the Dublin Horse Show and lost half a stone in weight and looked such an evil creature after two hours' sleep a night. I stayed in a house party and I never saw a horse the whole time. One came back from parties about lunchtime, had a couple of hours' sleep, and got prepared for the next party, with drinks beginning about 5 in the evening. The whole thing is a slight blur. I do remember having a bucket of ice from the champagne being poured over me at the Hibernian. I gatecrashed three hunt balls and was invited to two. It was very wicked and lots of fun.

Now, I can't imagine why the season should go on. It's all very well to have a nice bit of social life after you've left school, but quite frankly these days you have it whether you've left school or not. It's fun to have a dance, but not to turn it into such a business. I mean I didn't work for six months. It was all stylized, and it was a style which didn't really suit me, but there were moments of tremendous fun. People made an enormous effort and some splendid parties were given. There was terrific competition over the grade of champagne, which was sometimes quite abysmal, and over the marquees, and one was always going into rooms transformed into South Sea islands, with nets and shells. It was just at the beginning of discotheques, which started to change a lot of things.

Now it is over I suppose I am glad I did it, if only to have experienced it, although I don't think it gave me any advantages or any more self-confidence or insight. It was just part of growing up at that particular time at that particular level. Now it is totally unnecessary because one experiences those things anyway; people don't live a sheltered school-room existence being taught by governesses and meeting no-one. Not having met many young men before, it did give you that opportunity, although the men were excessively pompous and excessively dull. They were in it for a good time, a free meal and an awful lot of booze, and most of them would have admitted it. Hardly anyone married at the end of it, but 17 is far too young to marry anyway.'

Alex Galitzine still has not married. She went on to do an art course at the Victoria and Albert Museum and then got a job as box-office assistant at the Criterion. The next year she took a Cordon Bleu course which she thinks is invaluable and went to Switzerland to cook. Now she has gone off to open a bar in Majorca.

In 1964, the *Express* reported, there were 300 debs, about the same as the previous season, and some 150 dances. That meant, it estimated, about £225,000 spent on food and drink. Florists expected to take £100 from each deb's mother. Photographers charged £30 a sitting. Others who benefitted were the musicians, to the tune of about £40,000, while car-hire firms probably made £50,000 from the season.

When Georgina Denison came out a year later, little had changed:

'Everyone I knew seemed to be doing the season. I went to finishing school in Paris while my mother went to those awful lunch parties. She was horrified by the way people kept asking her what her daughter was like and then telling her how intelligent and beautiful their daughters were, and I think she feared when I arrived on the scene I would be quite the plainest and stupidest of the lot. But in the end she enjoyed it because she had always wanted to get a flat in London—we lived in Nottingham—and she persuaded my father to get one. She loved being in London and meeting all her friends after living in the country.

But I enjoyed it, even the tea parties, and the cocktail parties, where I was always rather going for the fathers; at that stage as they seemed far more interesting. Then there was the absurdity of Queen Charlotte's where the competition was to see who could get to Annabel's first. The dances were endlessly in the Hyde Park Hotel, which we slightly turned our noses up at because we knew it was the cheapest.

Already that year, the most glamorous people were saying, "Oh, no, we're not doing the season," and I don't think we took it very seriously although in many ways I was a very proper deb. I think it was a way of propping up a certain kind of society and also helping the worries of mothers like mine who knew their daughters would end up working in London. Ideally, she wanted me to meet the children of her friends. She would have said she wanted me to have a wide circle of friends, but in fact it was very narrow. I suppose I did stay within that kind of society until I was about 22, although I always seemed to have thoroughly undesirable boy-friends like Pakistani poets.

I was passionately in love with someone of 32 all through the season, so I wasn't remotely interested in the eligible young men. But the majority of people certainly weren't sleeping with anyone, or if you were, you were very discreet. I was certainly a virgin, though the girl I shared the flat with had been seduced by a man of about 40 and we were always having grilling sessions and asking what it was like: "No, it's not enough to say it's like a waterfall." But I think the boys were just as anguished about the whole thing as the girls. What fascinated me afterwards was that I got to know well two of the smoothest and sexiest young men, whom I had looked upon with a certain amount of suspicion. But I discovered that at that point, when they were about 22, neither of them had been to bed with a girl and it was all a big act. But we all thought they were going around seducing everybody. But I can remember the mystery of the fat plain girls who always used to go off at the end of the dance with the most attractive men.

And it was completely pre-drug. In general I suppose the Establishment is the slowest to catch up with change. By the time they had and didn't want to imitate their parents any more, the "glorious revolution" of the 1960s was almost over. But in an unheard-of way, we accepted our parents' views.

There were some marvellous dances and marvellous houses; Belvoir, Chatsworth and Burghley were all stunning, and I was so glad to see them all lit up with their ballrooms being used as ballrooms. You would get letters from a hostess you didn't know, and we had to invest in a Debrett so that we could look them up and see whether they were "Lady" or not, and still one got it wrong. The weekends were fantastic. Often there would be servants to unpack for you, which was always a bit embarrassing because of patched underclothes. When I was staying at Blenheim with my parents, my mother was horrified by the state of my underclothes and I was the only guest who didn't get brought breakfast in my room. The longer weekends, the servants would lay out what they thought you should wear and at that time it wasn't really as formal as the servants would have liked it to be. If you had planned to wear trousers for dinner, you would find they might lay out your night-gown as being the only hope for you.

I was nervous at the first dance I went to, and of course it was the worst. I was dancing with a man called Liechtenstein, and after we had got through the "How old are you?" I asked him where he lived. When he said, "Liechtenstein," I said, "How funny, is yours a common name, like Smith?" He said, "Not really. I am the Crown Prince."

I didn't madly enjoy my own dance, which was at Claridge's and shared with two girls. Rather sad, really, when you consider the expense, but it was quite late in the year and by then it felt a bit of a duty and just another London dance. I know the cost did cross my mind, because we had to chop down lots of trees to pay for it. My mother had been to see Jennifer to find out how the diary was, but in fact we forgot to tell her the date of ours, which apparently was a great *faux pas*. But publicity was a bit frowned on; there were whispers about those who were keen on it, and people would say, "Don't talk to Nigel Dempster, he works for William Hickey".

The men were a nice ordinary bunch of Old Etonians who were rather depressed because they had just started to become chartered accountants or to go into banks, and did not like the idea very much. What was very depressing, when you consider it was 1965, was that we knew so little and just took it for granted that the way to live was our parents' way. The season did give one a sense—a very false sense—of becoming a grown-up person. Suddenly everyone was making a fuss of you and you were known beyond your immediate circle. You were made to feel important but it was in your parents' world. And if you went to certain dances, like the one at Belvoir, you suddenly realised how scruffy the debs were and how splendid the mothers looked.

One gain I think was that it got one over being impressed by titles, smart houses and parties. But even one year later, I thought, "Look at those silly debs making such a fuss about their parties," and I was becoming increasingly embarrassed by the fact I had done the season because of the social aspect. One was horrified to discover that one had thought that was the entire world.'

Georgina went on to work at the National Book League and now runs the publicity department of publisher Victor Gollancz. She has a flat in Knightsbridge and bicycles to her office in Covent Garden. She is one of the very few debs who has a proper and highly successful career.

14

THE SEASON IN DECLINE

The season, by the second half of the 1960s, was in decline, whether it was the result of a Socialist government (as Peter Townend, now social editor of the *Tatler*, believes) or changing tastes (Max Colombi's theory) or simply a shortage of money. London had officially been dubbed the 'most exciting city' by American journalist John Crosby, writing in the *Daily Telegraph* colour supplement in 1965. London, he went on, was 'where the action is, the gayest, most uninhibited—and in a wholly new and very modern sense—the most coolly elegant city in the world.' The 'New Aristocrats' were pop stars like the Beatles and Mick Jagger. The image was classless, with emphasis on the lower-middle and working-class origins of photographers like David Bailey and Terence Donovan or actors Michael Caine and Terence Stamp. Debs no longer wanted to dance to Tommy Kinsman at Claridge's, they twisted at discotheques, talking in rather bad East End accents. British fashions swept the world and *Time* and *Newsweek* devoted articles to the new swinging image of London. In October 1965 the Thomson organization, in an attempt to tap this new society, replaced the old *Tatler* with the short-lived ultra-trendy *London Life*.

England may have been fashionable, but economically it was in a mess. In the March election of 1966, Labour had increased its majority to 97, but there were balance-of-payment problems and, in November of the next year, devaluation. This was followed by stringent currency controls and, in March 1968, the biggest tax increases in British history, with hefty taxes on capital and unearned income.

The *Daily Telegraph* reported one deb's mum as saying in April 1967, 'The season is marvellous if you do it in a small way. It's good for a girl before she goes to university, for example, much better than going straight from school. She has more poise.' That year, the *Telegraph* added, 'With the squeeze, the heat is off; but two years ago there were 400 girls and mothers paying £4,000 for them to come out. I am sure a lot of mothers are glad that it is better balanced.'

In Jean Rook's view, writing about the Berkeley Dress Show in the *Sun* the same month, '1967 is not a vintage year for debs. Only Miss Churchill and Lady Juliana Noel, daughter of the Earl of Gainsborough, are what I would call debs de luxe. Most of the others in the show tended to be good British stockbroking stock.' According to *The Times*'s early list of parties (inclusion was then 2 guineas) there were only to be 38 dances (17 in London), 27 cocktail parties and 8 charity balls.

'I don't think the end of presentations was really the death knell of the season,' reflects Peter Townend, 'I think it was when the Labour government came in with a big majority and there wasn't so much money around and everything toned down a

Page 154: By 1969, boutique-bought clothes were the order of the day for debutantes. Seen here is Lady Jane Wellesley, later tipped as a possible bride for Prince Charles, with Mr Bob Rodwell at a dance given by the Earl and Countess of Gainsborough for their daughter, Lady Maria Noel.

bit. Also the girls got more liberated. Today you would never get someone like Dr Rose Dugdale being ordered to come out by her mother. In the old days, when a girl was 18, she came out and that was that, whereas these days, the very grand girls, the titled girls, often don't come out in that sense at all. They will simply have a private party for the people they know. I think you can never know enough people and there's not much point in having a party for the people you know.'

Peter Townend, by writing to remind mothers that their daughters are now of a suitable age to do the season, has made a big contribution to its perilous survival:

'The season as such doesn't change, because the events—Ascot, the Fourth of June—are still there. But the participation of debutantes has changed. At one time, any girl of 18 of a certain social strata came out at 18 and did nothing else but come out. Nowadays there is hardly a debutante who is a debutante and nothing else. But the girls still do see it as a means of meeting new people and that is still its most important aspect, although generally it is girl-friends they make. It does not seem to be a marriage market any more, but then these days there are other chances of them meeting their future husbands, whereas in the old days, the only chance a girl had was during the season.

But now it has become so expensive. Taking everything into consideration— clothes, travel, Ascot, charity ball tickets, drinks parties, dinner parties and your own dance—you couldn't get away with much less than £20,000, probably more. It is a very large sum, and people have considerable difficulty in breaking family trusts to get it. If there is only one daughter it might be possible, but if there are several you could not possibly do it. Now there are certainly far fewer dances.

No one would attempt to do the season now unless they knew a couple of people. You have to know a nucleus to begin with, otherwise the girl would just be un-comfortable. More often, there are cocktail parties instead of dances. The cocktail parties used to be just in the beginning of the season to get people meeting one another, whereas now they have them in the autumn and even in December when there's no more excitement about them. And for the men that makes it so different. It used to be said that a man could live for weeks on end without buying himself a meal, whereas now the boot's on the other foot and the man is expected to take the girl out after a cocktail party.

The parties are not so grand and the dresses are far simpler. You would never get a Dior creation. There are very few parties where there is proper champagne, it is nearly always sparkling wine. And though they are called cocktail parties, they very rarely serve anything in the way of cocktails. At one time if you went to a cocktail party, there was gin, whisky, everything on the tray, whereas now there is just some champagne-type drink plus either orange juice or tomato juice on the tray. If you look a bit older, as I do, the waiter may tell you there is something stronger, but they keep the whisky and stuff behind the scenes.

Titles are still valuable, even in our egalitarian age, but the girls if they are dull and plain are not much in demand even if they are titled. Often, I think, it is the dull ones who are keener to do the season because they hope it will broaden their field, whereas their prettier friends will have gone to parties already and know lots of people. I was very surprised when one mother said to me the other day that she would not let her daughter accept invitations because she was coming out the next year, but it depends on the mothers and on the girls. Lady Antonia Fraser's two elder daughters have been around for ages. But some girls are sophisticated at 16 and others are shy at 20, and no matter how liberated things may become, that does not change.

There are still weekend parties but now you are lucky if your hostess meets you at the station. People are finding house parties too expensive, entertaining ten people you don't know and whom you don't like and who may not like you. I know one lady who always used to have them says they are now too expensive. Even in 1970 I can remember a host whispering to me that he was not going to get out the port and that every one could just have another glass of wine because it was too dear, and then prices were not as bad as they are now. People still do go to things in Scotland but not Ireland any more, partly because the bank holiday has changed and it doesn't coincide with the Horse Show any longer, partly the troubles, but mainly the cost.

I suppose if money becomes easier it might revive again, but it is hard to think there could be a dance like, for example, the one at Upton Park for Felicity Samuel in 1966 which was meant to have cost £100,000. That was very grand; all the rooms were lined, there was a pub, a marquee, Chris Barber. In the past three years the numbers of dances has gone right down. I should think the grandest this year was the one at the Berkeley given by the Sassoons, and that was for only 180 people. I hope the season can carry on because everything today is so grey that one does appreciate a bit of glamour.'

From his vantage point as banqueting manager of the Dorchester from 1943 till his retirement in 1970, Max Colombi makes this comment: 'By the 1960s, there was a gradual decline in the general style of private dances. With the growing popularity of the Beatles' type of music, ballroom dancing was becoming unfashionable and sound was amplified to such an extent that the parents and older guests withdrew to quieter rooms. Also the general behaviour of both the young men and girls became *blasé* and ill-mannered, quite unacceptable to many of the hostesses.' Or, as Tommy Kinsman puts it, 'The kids wanted to do the opposite to what their parents did. They called everything old-fashioned.'

Ian McCorquodale, son of romantic novelist Barbara Cartland, attributes the decay of the season to both the change in styles and of sexual permissiveness:

'Ours was not a permissive age, and people did not leap in and out of bed. I don't think we even thought about it very much. We used to stay up late to dance, whereas now I suppose they shuffle off to bed at about midnight. Debs will never

Below: Snob value helps to promote a new brand of petrol. Seen here are debutantes (from right) Miss Roxana Lampson, Miss Anne Dunhill, Miss Nikki Phillips, Miss Carolyne Houston, Miss Fiona Hughes, Miss Moranna Cazanove, Miss Rosemary Walduck, Miss Lucy Jane Maturin Cameron, and Miss Olivia Smithers. Right: A very formal Princess Anne escorted by Mr Charles Fforde at the Caledonian Ball in 1969. Below right: The word 'debutante' had disappeared from the Berkeley Dress Show's title by 1973.

The
Berkeley Dress Show

*

The Berkeley
on
Monday 9th April 1973

*

IN AID OF THE
National Society for the Prevention of Cruelty to Children

The
Berkeley Debutante Dress Show

*

The Savoy
on
Monday April 13th 1970 at 4 p.m.
Tuesday April 14th 1970 at 11.30 a.m.

*

IN AID OF THE
The Prevention of Cruelty to Children

Far right: Debutantes chosen to model in the 1969 Berkeley Dress Show are given helpful hints at the Lucie Clayton Model School. Right: Still glamorous in 1976, Lady Diana Cooper and Margaret, Duchess of Argyll accompany Miss Elizabeth Brewer at a ball.

come back if they are popping into bed when they are 17, because they won't want to go to dances. In my day it was much more romantic. You would dance with a girl and take her out a few times before you even kissed her.

I view the season with a certain degree of nostalgia and I am sad it has disappeared, because I think it was a traditional part of England and a good launching-pad for the girls, making sure they would meet the most eligible people. Now one will have to make sure one's daughters go to the right school.

I think the whole thing started to deteriorate when we stopped wearing white ties and began to shuffle round in dinner jackets. White ties were difficult and never really comfortable, but one did feel smart and it did add a certain degree of glamour. Then suddenly it was the pop age and long hair, and everything was different. When I was at Cambridge, everyone wore sports jackets, cavalry twill trousers and short brushed and clean hair. We would have thought people with long hair were queer. Somehow the change led to sexual permissiveness. But perhaps it will change back. More people than ever are reading my mother's books. She always says that permissiveness is the woman's fault and that men get bored if they can have it the first night. The chase is more fun.'

More seriously, Nigel Dempster sees the disappearance of the season as part of the inevitable loss of their old power by the upper classes, largely through their own stupidity and lack of foresight. Speaking in 1976, he said:

'I think the old social order was reprehensible. I cannot tell you my loathing of it. It was based on the old upper-middle-class wheeze of keeping yourself to yourself, which is why Annabel's still exists, and saving your daughters from any yahoo

160

who might come along. Now the class is decimated and they are having to sell their houses, and they are left with foolish, ugly, ill-educated girls, still wearing their old Hermes editions. It was the upper classes trying to perpetuate their hoax upon the world to keep themselves to themselves.

There was a gradual decline, and then in 1973 the dances vanished completely, although there will always be someone to give a dance. Mrs Harmsworth did in 1974 for her daughters Geraldine and Sarah Brooks, which was a good party because it was a mixture of people, from Rex Harrison to Charles Clore. It was different from the old days because now one knows everyone who is there. But the last good year was 1958. By 1965 a lot had already changed, and then by 1967 you hardly found anyone drinking except for people like me. It was sex and drugs. Everyone else was smoking exotic cheroots. The parents must have been aware what was happening. A father's drinks bill for a dance must have been minimal. People no longer wore dinner jackets, they came in whatever they were wearing. It was the pop revolution.

But when I did the season I enjoyed it and was grateful that I was allowed to do it. I am Australian and was brought up to believe that what mattered was the English ruling class, which was the upper class. It was a halcyon life for me, a vast experience, coming from a backwater in Australia where five was a crowd and after being fairly horrified by British public schools. By the age of 24 I had had the privilege of dining with people like Macmillan, Douglas-Home and Reggie Maudling. I knew the five senior people in the government. Now the Tory party is in total disarray and will not recover. The landed gentry are in total disarray.

They have nothing left to sell, they have been foolishly educated. Most were encouraged to finish their education at an early age. I am now 34, and 70 per cent of the men I knew when I was doing the season still do not have jobs, in the age-group 26 to 36. They were told they would not have to work because of trust funds or that there would always be some cushy job available. Now the income from their trust funds won't keep them in sarsaparilla and there are no jobs. They thought they would be insulated from the future, but now they are dependent on people like me to pick up the bills at lunch. It was the result of foolish people marrying foolish people. In the late 1950s, there was still a lot of antisemitism; Evelyn de Rothschild had a hard time at dances because he was a Jew. Fulham is populated with girls in their early thirties with two children whose marriages haven't lasted—the clink of Gucci on the pavements is like an army—they have no training or education, they can't afford nannies and they have to face a future where the children go not to Eton but to somewhere more mundane.

Sometimes you see the upper classes in a last desperate attempt to prove nothing is changed. In January I went to a party the Hartingtons gave where the band was Old Etonian; for all I know the waiters might have been Old Etonians. Annabel's is their last refuge. It is the last place where you can see the double-breasted dinner jacket and the crumpled trousers. They used to be able to afford to go anywhere, but what you notice as time goes on is that these children like Alexander Rufus Isaacs can't afford to go out. At Annabel's and Tramp, very few people are under 25 unless they are pop stars or in the music business, which is the new aristocracy. The others can't afford a bill of £20. There will always be some people who have money, if your name is Astor, and the three Heskeths were left five million between them, but people are beginning to be ashamed of spending money. If they do spend money and are caught out by me, it embarasses them more, especially since columns like mine are read avidly by the Inland Revenue. The wind of change is blowing through the bank accounts of the rich. But for old times' sake I will sometimes write a piece in the diary about one of their marriages breaking up, or I will spend a day at Cowes or walk through the Guards' Polo Club.

They are an endangered species, and Mrs Betty Kenward is the lightning conductor through which they communicate. It is horrendous to think she considers her diary a "record of life". If the Martians only read that, they would think Britain was inhabited by freaks and perverts. She is a free-loader, but you do have to admire her energy, and I expect she is worth about 10,000 circulation to *Harpers' Queen*.

But I am glad I was in at the end of the season; it is like going to see a dinosaur and remembering it with flesh and when it walked. It gave me an ability to get on with people—you have to be able to if you sit next to Macmillan for two hours when you are 24. Looking around now, as Somerset Maugham said, the only pleasure of growing old is to see the downfall of one's contemporaries.'
Lady Diana Cooper reflected on the changes:
'The rich have gone down enormously. The change in my living standards has been something grotesque. On paper, it is completely different and one doesn't even dare use the words "standard of living"; it doesn't do. I was not born into riches—indeed we were quite poor until my father succeeded—but one was always

served. There is no service today. I have a darling Portuguese maid who is a first-class dressmaker, but she cannot cook, so I either eat out or bring something back.

But everything is so different. I have a granddaughter and she would never have bothered to come out. She went to Oxford and now she is doing Voluntary Service Overseas in Alexandria. It would seem ridiculous to me today.

The only dance I've been to lately was given by one of Lady Lambton's daughters who is my god-daughter, to entertain Andy Warhol—that was hardly a debutante dance. There was nothing there but freaks.'

Andrew Maconie, another Old Etonian who still occasionally appears in Jennifer's Diary as a tycoonish figure, remembers:

'I had a competition when I was doing the season thing with a very smooth man who also worked in advertising to see who could get into the magazines more often, and I won with three *Tatlers* and two *Queens*. But the world I live in is now quite different. I lunch at Morton's, and if I look round who's there? Half the girls are models, the rest are pop stars. Then there's Nigel Dempster, and I would say at the most five per cent are deb types. The last stronghold is Annabel's. If you go there at least half a dozen people from school will be there, but it is by no means the "Hullo-how-are-you" place it was. Now you are taken more on your merits than on where you were at school, which is a good thing.

But the season was good in my day and I enjoyed it. You were dropped into it and it was up to you whether you sank or swam. Some girls may have had a miserable time, but that was her fault. Sure, some girls are less attractive than others. It is up to them to make more of themselves.'

Even the few official seasonal functions recognized the change and in 1971 Queen Charlotte's Ball dropped the word 'debutante' from its title, although there were still the Maids of Honour curtseying to Queen Charlotte's representative. As Sylvia Darley put it in 1976, 'We think of it as a Hospital Ball. It is a shop window for the hospital and at the moment we cannot think of a better way to raise £3,000. There is no longer a ballot to select the Maids of Honour, but all who take part in the procession must wear white and they must be able to come to the rehearsal in the morning. Last year there were 116 in the procession, which was quite a good number to manage.' The girls made their curtsey to a varied selection of peeresses, including the Duchess of Northumberland, the Duchess of Rutland and Princess Anne of Denmark. 'Whoever is kind enough to do it,' Sylvia Darley explained, 'it is a chore getting one's jewels out of the bank and bringing a party, but so far I have always been able to persuade one of my friends to do it.'

It had been harder in recent years to get sufficient debutantes interested in the season, partly because, Richard Berens says, 'The girls have dropped out because they been learning to become human beings and to contribute to the tax-man. In the old days, they never really did any proper jobs. They simply took silly little jobs to keep them occupied, rather than for the money.'

In any case, if parents were going to spend money on their daughters, they wanted to get good value. 'Now people realize,' commented Countess Zamoyska, 'that it is a better investment to spend their money renting a chalet in Switzerland or a villa in the South of France—something people really enjoy—than to pay the larger cost of the doubtful investment in a large ball in London.'

15
THE PRESENT-DAY DEB

Since daughters no longer want to do the season and fathers are not able to afford the luxury, or doubt the value of the exercise, it is surprising how many remnants of the old coming-out days have survived. Yet the lifestyle of the modern deb does pose the question of whether she is a deb in anything but name. Jennifer stopped listing private dances in 1975 (on the grounds that as in war days, it is no longer a good idea to publicise private parties) although *The Times* still carry their list, inclusion costing £6 for one entry in 1976. The last two lists Jennifer published do illustrate how the numbers of private parties had declined. In 1973, Jennifer listed 18 cocktail parties between 10 May and 12 December and twenty dances between 26 May and 22 December, of which fourteen were in the country and only six in London. Several of the parties doubled as 21st birthday parties for another member of the family. Slightly petulantly, Jennifer said, 'I would appreciate it tremendously if mothers would cut out my list and keep it for reference. This, I hope, will lessen the numerous telephone calls to my office'. She did not bother to ask this in 1974 when there were nineteen cocktail parties in her list and twenty-four dances. But only three were in London, or four if you count Wimbledon.

Mrs Betty Kenward (Jennifer) thinks that it was the alteration in educational formulas which has been one of the biggest influences on the debutante season. As more girls take examinations in June, they are too busy to go to parties in what used to be the peak deb months of May and June so that more goes on in July. Because of the economic situation, the parties tend to be smaller and there are more cocktail parties than dances. Nonetheless, she feels it is still beneficial for the girls and that it does give them a chance to meet people and to see how people live.

The return to power of the Tories in 1970 seems to have had little effect, but with Heath and his 'Selsdon Man' image this is hardly surprising. Popular press interest in debutantes has diminished, although the term ex-deb is still a useful one to attach to a figure in a scandal. Occasionally the papers will take an almost sociological look at the debutante. In 1974 both the *Observer* and the *Evening Standard* took the attitude of an anthropologist commenting on a rare tribe. Michael Whale in the *Standard* interviewed one of the 1974 Berkeley debs, Katherine Percy, daughter of ex-Lonrho executive Gerald Percy. He quoted Katherine as saying, 'Before I started the season, people did say, "What are you going to do next year?" and when I said that I'd got to stay in London because of the season, they gave me such an odd look. There is a stigma attached to the word deb. Wasting money, I think, is a big point people make. I think that people who don't know a lot about it think, "What a lot of money spent on parties and socialising".' Mr Percy was, however, reluctant to divulge any costs to Michael Whale.

By now the Berkeley Dress Show had followed Queen Charlotte's in leaving out 'debutante' from its name. The *Observer* reported on 28 April 1974:

'The opening shots of what used to be the deb season were heard in London last week with the Berkeley Dress Show. Once it was a pleasant enough way for the cream of the debs to show themselves off. Now it has become a highly commercial operation to show the clothes off.

Twenty years ago the Season was the way babes from the best families were launched into Society, and on to the marriage market. There was some social test—the Lord Chamberlain still scrutinised would-be debs for presentation at Court—and the rest of the season revolved round this ritual.

When the Presentations stopped in 1968, a pale imitation of this selection process hinged on Queen Charlotte's Ball, a public charity affair, held in a hotel, but with carefully vetted entry (vetted by whom was never quite certain). This year for the first time, all pretensions have been dropped. Anyone with £8 to spend on a dinner-dance ticket can get in. Dropping the barriers has been good for business.

Even before this final *coup de grâce*, the Season had become more commercial than social. Aristocrats and diplomats gave way to company directors and bankers. It actually caused a stir when the 18-year-old Duke of Marlborough's heir, the Marquess of Blandford, was spotted at a dance earlier this month.

Parents are still pouring thousands into marquees, bands and cocktail catering. But it's more with the unabashed object of enjoying what their money can bring and entertaining their friends than with the single-minded purpose of off-loading cloistered young ladies into marriage. Most young ladies these days are no longer cloistered. They have their own ideas about their lives and it doesn't necessarily involve a quick safe marriage. Social values have changed, even though the dance goes on.'

The *Observer* was right to say parents would need to pour their money into marquees and bands: today a large marquee, 105 feet by 40 feet, would cost £6,000; to hire a band like the Autocrats would be £500 while the more traditional Joe Loss would cost something like £800.

In 1975, press comment on debutantes was restricted to speculation as to whether or not Queen Charlotte's Ball would survive because the tickets were so slow in selling. Anne Thomas, one of that year's debs, was asked to go on Radio 4's *Newsbeat* to explain that she and her friends were not just rich young ladies having a nice time but that all her friends were also studying or working, and that the real point was to raise money for the hospital. But times had changed since the enchanted days of 1959, when the committee had to turn down 300 applications for tickets.

The worries of the committee did not, however, bother young men like Charles Miskin, for whom there were still a lot of parties to go to. His sister was one of those who half-did the season and he started to go to dances when he was at Oxford in 1970. In 1975 he stopped because he was working rather harder as a pupil barrister:

'Things have changed enormously in the past five years. Now, the true deb thing has ended; now it is just parties, and everybody has parties whether they are terribly rich or terribly poor. But there is no special significance or *cachet* about so-called deb parties. But even in the beginning I was a little disappointed, having seen lots of those delicious Rex Harrison films about the kind of party that went on in the 1950s, and I was surprised to discover they were no more and no less than glorified discotheque parties and rather boring cocktail parties. But I did once go to one of those famous tea parties, and when we got there hundreds of girls were sitting around with their address books open and their afternoon party dresses on, desperately trying to be grown-up and failing on every conceivable ground.

And Queen Charlotte's Ball, which I have been to twice, which is enough for any man. It is a mixture, somewhere between the Nuremberg Rallies and the Dance of the Fairies in the Hall of the Mountain King, with this procession of what could be Hitler Youth dressed up in white and parading down to curtsey to some fantastically third-rate piece of foreign royalty who graciously receives the cake which nobody eats, as far as I can see. It's mesmeric in its stupidity: half the girls are whimpering in anticipation of this great event, as though they were about to be confirmed; for the rest, you can see they would be far happier in the saddle than wearing a white party dress. The first year I went they had introduced a discotheque, so after the fathers had had their first dance with their daughters, I was forced to go upstairs to this absurd discotheque where I sweated, I really sweated, because tails and boiled shirts are not ideally suited to dancing to fast music. That kind of party is bound to be a bit oppressive because you have the parents as well. My sister did not bother to do it.

The cocktail parties are awful. They entice you into some delightful club where you get served up with champagne and just when you're expecting great things, suddenly at 8.30, the champagne dries up and you spend the next quarter of an hour hunting around for half-filled glasses other people have left. Then it comes to an end and there you are, *bam!*—let down, unfulfilled, dissatisfied.

Peter Townend and I never saw quite eye-to-eye, but I was on the unofficial network of acquaintanceship which is a far more powerful lever than any list.'

This Roneoed list, incidentally, encouraged the belief that not too much has changed. Of the 120 suitable young men in 1975, there were four Lords, an Earl and a Duke, sufficient Hons. and Baronets to encourage the young ladies, while the surnames—Wyndham, Somerset, Wellesley, Charteris—are those which would have circulated in the 1930s.

Despite the preponderance of cocktail parties over dances, Charles Miskin did not find his involvement with the deb season expensive:

'It was really five years of free-loading. In the time I've been doing it, the girls

167

change but the men remain the same, just looking a little older with a few more wrinkles and getting plump and well-established in the City. The men are the ones who are thinking of marrying and settling down, whereas the girls disappear off to somewhere like East Africa to be secretaries. You do meet lots of glorious debs from yesteryear doing very simple things like working in shops, and you remember them having a dance which cost £25,000. I think the girls who do the season properly tend to be the ones who are not very clever; the nicer ones are those who are not debs at all but simply go to the occasional party given by a friend.

Scotland is much more old-fashioned. The best organized party I went to was in Roxburghshire, but in Scotland everyone is always on their best behaviour and there were even people patrolling upstairs to see that nothing went on. It was frightfully dull. They are still very staid up there and worry about their daughters. And in Ireland the parties go on for days, it's a real razzle, although everyone is very tough and gets up to go riding in the morning. One dance I went to, Prime Minister Liam Cosgrave's daughter was there staying the night and her two guards slept across the entrance to her room like Indian body-servants.

What I enjoyed most were the dinner parties, which are fairly formal, and it is of some importance to your hostess that you should turn up at least in a dinner jacket. But now I am taking my work more seriously and haven't the time to go on to Annabel's, which is expensive and dull, or Raffles, which is middle-aged. If Annabel's is for the rich middle-aged, Raffles is for the poor middle-aged. Then of course there is the gorgeous François's, to which I always owe an awful lot of money and where I don't suppose I shall go much more because it is a club which appeals to those from 17 to 22. Then people seem to fade away, apart from a couple of relics hanging around. I walk in there and see one or two old friends and we lean on the bar and talk to the proprietor.

There are the girls who don't go to bed with every man on sight and there are those who do, but certainly if a girl has been out with someone for a certain amount of time she will probably sleep with him, and there is not much her parents can do, unless they collect their little darling from every dance she goes to. What is curious, or curiouser as Alice would say, is that any do still get pregnant because of birth control.

What there is, far more than the mothers suspect, is drugs. Mothers probably expect their daughters to go to bed with somebody but what they don't realize is how easy it is for them to get drugs. Most of the girls do take drugs, though not on a regular basis; there are not fantastic drug addicts. But rich young girls are easy prey for rich young men who get richer selling drugs. But the girls are very unspoilt, really, and the true deb is a fairly dull creature because she has no other impulse.

There's always a shortage of men, so that if you are reasonably respectable it is easy to get invited. The men tend to be eternally in insurance or stockbroking, not many in the army, plus one or two who are frightfully rich and don't do anything. To the mothers, provided your hair is cut and you can play tennis, it doesn't really matter who you are. Say some mother caught her darling daughter in bed with some man in the house, I think her reaction would be, "For God's sake, don't do it here; what would your father say?". Whereas I think the father probably knows but doesn't bother to look.'

Anne Thomas, who was one of the very few debutantes to have a London dance in 1975, not surprisingly takes a less sardonic view than Charles Miskin. She did the season with thoroughness and enjoyment, attitudes shared by her mother. Anne is the elder daughter of baronet Sir Michael Thomas, a stockbroker, and she is thus very much from the background which produced the post-war debutante. Yet her mother, Lady (Meg) Thomas, doubts whether the season can survive and says she and her husband only decided to give Anne a season after discussing several other alternatives. She has no thought of bringing out her younger daughter, whom she expects to go to university. Lady Thomas herself came out in 1952:

'I didn't do the season in a big way because my mother refused to come up from Kent. Anne did it in a much bigger way because I worked harder. But I remember well it was the year the King died, and being presented was a bit of a problem because of what to wear. In the end I had a chocolate lace dress which my mother thought would be appropriate. I went to Mme Vacani to learn to curtsey, but it didn't make much difference, because I had water on the knee and it creaked and creaked and I couldn't get up and Prince Philip had an enormous smile on his face.

My mother had this great horror of taxis because she had this great thing about debs' delights being not safe in taxis. If the dance were at a hotel she would literally book a room for me there so I did not have to get into a taxi with a man. It didn't occur to her that my having a room might be far less safe. With Anne, what I used to worry about was drinking and driving because the young drink so much these days, and she would come back so terribly late after a cocktail party, then dinner and then a nightclub. The one thing we said was that Anne must telephone us so that we would know how late she would be.'

But unless, as in Anne's year, energetic mothers get together to make sure the season continues, Lady Thomas finds it hard to see that it can keep going:

'I think it is rather sad and that in some ways the point of the season has gone. We offered Anne lots of things before the season, but then Peter Townend wrote to me and said that they were terribly short of people and as Anne was living at home, why not let her do it? At that stage there were only about 60 girls, but in the end I think there were 180. I had not really thought about it before and in any case I thought Anne might be on the shy side to do it, but she turned out to be one of the extroverts, which was quite extraordinary.

But on the whole, children are rebelling and are put off it because everything is swinging to the Left. I don't think any girl would do it who was going to university or had a definite vocation, but Anne's not a career girl and she was a bit young to travel with any confidence, so it was nice to have a year of nothing serious.'

During the year, Anne, like many of her friends, was doing a cookery course; she was at Mrs Pomeroy's. Others were doing secretarial courses and some their A-levels, which Lady Thomas considered a mistake because she thought it put them under too much pressure. Unusually, no one from Anne's school was doing the season. 'In fact,' she admitted, 'people would tend to say, "So-and-so's going to do the season, she must be a real snob," whereas a couple of years ago a lot did it.'

'This year,' Lady Thomas explained, 'there were mainly cocktail parties, often three or four a night. There were hardly any London dances, which is why we

169

Far left: Lord Hesketh and Miss Pamela Tennant at Queen Charlotte's Ball in 1971. Left: Mr Charles Miskin and Miss Emma Laidlaw at a party given by Viscount and Viscountess Sandon for their son's 21st birthday and their daughter's coming-out. Below far left: A view of the Caledonian Ball in 1970. Below centre: Mr Charles Camp, one of the young men on 'the list', with Miss Emily Kark at the Moth Ball in 1977. Below: Four of the debs helping plan the 1977 Berkeley Dress Show were (seated) Lady Mountain, Miss Charlotte Czernine, Miss Georgina Mountain, and (standing) Miss Caroline Greenish.

were determined to give her one. It was tremendous fun. We had it at Hurlingham, which is just round the corner. I was very keen on a band but the girls—she shared it with Lenore Campbell—did not want that, so we had a discotheque, and the club had its own nightclub. But we had a lot of gate-crashers including Caroline Kennedy in her blue jeans which I told her off about. I told her I knew she had only been in England a week but jeans are really not the thing if you are going to crash somebody's party. We had invited 400 but we reckon at least 500 came. People had to bring their invitations and we stood in the receiving line from 9.30 till about 11, when we were dropping, and the gate-crashers came after that. The most embarassing thing were the ones we knew but had not invited.'

Lady Thomas admits to having enjoyed herself enormously:

'The lunch parties were to my mind tremendous fun, absolutely terrific. It was with school-friends, people like that, and people very much doing it on a shoestring, which was rather nice. We all came to the conclusion we must not spend too much. When I had mine I had about thirty people, it was easier like that. I remember meeting Lady Paget's husband and apparently—they have rather a small house—she had given thirteen luncheon parties. I didn't like to tell him I had been to two.

For the date of the dance, I saw Betty [Kenward] and discussed it with her and saw what was in the diary. Then we discussed it with Peter [Townend] and arranged a date when nothing was on. That was in about February. Betty said it was going to be a very slim year indeed and she didn't think people were making a big enough effort at all. One bit of advice she did give me was not to let Anne go in for the Berkeley Dress Show, because she said if there were ever any trouble in the future she would always get into the headlines as a Berkeley deb, and that it would dog her for the rest of her life. But I went on the committee and Anne went on the junior committee and we helped run it. Anne was very good about helping with charity things, which I think is something they do learn from the season.

I don't really know where the myth of the season costing so much comes from. You have to do various things like having two lunch parties and about two tea parties, and you have to budget for the Berkeley Dress Show and Queen Charlotte's, some charity dances and dinners, plus the dance and Ascot, but we would have given her a coming-of-age party at 18 anyway, and it was just a question of sharing it with the Campbells instead of having more people. We had a lovely party for Queen Charlotte's, sixteen young people and twelve of us, and Anne was lent a marvellous Norman Hartnell dress.'

The debutantes themselves were less happy about having to wear white to Queen Charlotte's. 'Some of them made their dresses,' said Anne, 'but I know Diana Washington's cost £50 and I don't think she has worn it since. But I did enjoy the ball.'

The first cocktail party Anne went to was the one given by Peter Townend, but before that she had been to lots of tea parties. 'One of the advantages of Mrs Pomeroy's,' explained her mother, 'was she finished in time to go to the tea parties. One of the main things is to encourage them to go to those, because that is where they meet their friends.'

'At the first one,' remembers Anne, 'I didn't know anyone and we all sat on the floor and had iced coffee, but then it gradually got off the ground. We were all very nervous at Peter's cocktail party, but he was very kind. Nobody knew anybody and Peter was marvellous at introducing us all. But when I met one man, Charles Camp it was, he struck me as being a typical deb's delight because he kept saying "When is your dance?" and "Are you inviting me?" and I did not even know his name. People were all trying to suck up to get invited and they would tell you you were the most beautiful girl in the room and one knew it was because they wanted invitations. But on the whole everyone was very nice and I have made some really good friends.'

Most of the young men were Lloyd's, City or university, but no army, rather to Lady Thomas's regret:

'The army seems to have completely faded. That was what we used to draw on. There are a few spongers, of course, but now it seems to me it is quite expensive for the boys because they have to take the girls out to dinner, and on to a night club afterwards. I am amazed how generous the boys have been. And the mothers of the boys have been marvellous and given lots of dances. What amazed me was how it was the young men that seemed to want to get married. Anne, darling, you had two proposals.'

'Only because I had an advanced cookery diploma.'

'A lot of the debs did not really give anything this year, but I think it is rather bad to accept if you are not going to invite back. As it was so much smaller this year, I think everybody did know everybody. Parents didn't go to things much but I don't think you want to have too many grown-ups. One dance we went to there were so many that they took up all the tables and chairs and there was literally nowhere for the teenagers to sit, and they love sitting and talking; they don't get dancing for ages. For our dance we only asked people like god-parents and relations. We gave a dinner first for about fifty people, and the Campbells did the same. We tried to get most people into dinner parties, especially the ones we were a bit worried about like Anne's school-friends and family friends. We had champagne at home, but at the dance we just had those very large bottles of wine which we bought and the club very kindly stored for us so we only had to pay corkage.'

Their dance was late in the year, in October, when Anne had her eighteenth birthday. This date apparently was rather a good one, because in July there were so many cocktail parties that they had all got rather tired:

'The trouble was you said you would go to too many, and then you tried to arrange to go to the one you thought would be best last of all—but sometimes you found you had the order wrong. I used to go with Lenore, who shared the dance. She had a car and we went everywhere together. We used to be called the Gruesome Twosome. Sometimes it was awful. We went to one cocktail party at the Guards' Club where we hadn't intended to stay long, but it was dreadful because there was no one there and the poor parents were wondering what had gone wrong. Generally you would go out to dinner and then to François's, which seemed to be *the* place, though I think Raffles is slightly cheaper. Membership is about £25. François's really is full of little Etonians, great fun, everyone is about 18.

Then I loved the house parties because I love the country. It was marvellous having a dance and then staying on to play tennis on Sunday. And I loved the Fourth of June . . .'

'I don't,' interrupted Lady Thomas, 'because all the men I know are Harrow.'

'What was marvellous,' said Anne, 'was I did meet so many people. I used to be frightfully shy and now I have so much more self-confidence.'

The only complaint Lady Thomas had was that she had to nag Anne to get her to write her bread-and-butter letters, something she would have done automatically when she was a deb. 'But one thing—doing the season definitely brings a mother and daughter closer together.'

The year 1976 wasn't exactly a prime one for debs. Some 100 curtsied at Queen Charlotte's Ball. Newspapers still wrote stories asking, 'Whatever happened to the Debs?' and the same deb's mum, Mrs Denis Drury, was interviewed continually. As she told the *Daily Mail*, 'It's really educational for all the family. The children learn an awful lot—how to behave with people and how to get on with them, and it's such fun.' But even she admitted the season was becoming less important. Her dance for her daughter Ruth was for 200 people, but it was held in December, which in former years would not have been considered a proper time for a debutante dance. But as Mrs Drury confided to another paper, 'One simply must go on giving parties in the old style. It teaches the girls such a lot and you know they are meeting the right kind of boy.' In 1977, even Queen Charlotte's Ball finally came to an end.

In 1976 only fourteen private cocktail parties and dances were listed; in 1977 it was nine. Peter Townend isn't too despondent. He thinks Queen Charlotte's could have been made to work and suggests that the Rose Ball may gradually take its place. 'The chairman is the granddaughter of Lady Howard de Walden, who started Queen Charlotte's, and she's bringing out her daughter this year and is getting all the debutantes to go to that.'

Certainly there will still be suitable marriages between the children of the so-called upper classes—Patrick Lichfield may have swanned around with models and film stars, but his bride was the daughter of the Duke of Westminster (although that had nothing to do with her being a debutante). The pretence that being a deb is anything special has collapsed. The ending of presentations at court may have had no immediate effect, but once they had gone, there was nothing to bolster the theory of the debutante.

INDEX

Page numbers in *italics* refer to illustrations